WIN
THE
FIGHT

THE FIGHT FORE MY LIFE

JEREMY GANT

www.xulonpress.com

My dearest Ashli,

Words can't describe how much you mean to me. The last year has been so memorable & I can't wait to create even more memories. Here's to forever!

I love you!!,

Jeremy Gant

This book is dedicated to everyone who supported me throughout my journey back to life, especially:

Our Lord Jesus Christ, for my belief and trust in His will is why I am here today.

My Mom and Dad, for always being there by my side and supporting me in whatever I do.

All of my family and friends, as they are always there for me–no matter what.

All of my doctors and nurses who kept me going along the way.

The community, especially those who prayed for me, as I couldn't have gotten through this without you.

Everyone who contributed to the Jeremy Gant Foundation, as all of your donations and help is truly appreciated.

Coach Notey, the Newman Golf Team and all the Newman community, for supporting me the whole way.

Coach McGraw, Rickie Fowler, Morgan Hoffmann, Taylor Gooch, the Oklahoma State Golf Team, Erik Compton and Tom Watson, for making my dreams come true.

Table of Contents

"Moreover, I will give you a new heart and put a new spirit within you; and I will remove the heart of stone from your flesh and give you a heart of flesh."

Ezekiel 36:26

Chapter One

The Start of It All

"**W**hat's happening?" I thought as I was moving my things up the stairs to my room for my second year at college. My roommates Kaleb and Nick noticed it, too.

"Dude, are you okay? You look like you just ran a marathon," Kaleb asked.

I replied, "Man I don't know what's going on. I'm exhausted..."

Keep in mind I had just won a bodybuilding contest and was in the best shape of my life. Feeling like this made no sense to me at all. Lately, I had been short of breath doing even ordinary activities like walking to class or carrying my golf bag.

After my friends noticed, I called my mom and asked what she thought I should do. We scheduled a doctor's appointment back in my hometown and decided to go from there.

When I arrived in Chanute, Mom and I went to the doctor's office and sat down in the waiting room.

"Mom, what do you think is wrong?" I asked. "I work out every day and this just doesn't make any sense."

"Jeremy, everything is going to be fine, I'm sure it's nothing major," she said. "They will probably just put you on some medication and that'll fix you right up." She smiled reassuringly.

When my name was called, we entered the exam room and explained what had been happening.

"I'll just be walking to class and by the time I get there, I'm completely winded," I told the doctor. "It just doesn't add up. And then sometimes I can feel my heart doing funny things, especially when I'm lying in bed at night."

"Hmm, well I agree," said Dr. Lee, my regular doctor in Chanute. "You're in excellent shape so this shouldn't be a problem. Let's take a listen to you." Lub-dup, lub-dup, lub-dup.

"Jeremy, it sounds normal but we better have you take a chest x-ray and make sure it's nothing to do with the heart," he said. And that's what we did.

Before I go any further I should probably give you a little history about myself. Ever since I was a little kid, I had dreamed of becoming a professional golfer. I wanted to compete against the greats like Tiger Woods and Phil Mickelson. As soon as I hit my first golf ball at the age of two, I was hooked. My dad, Cecil, would take me out to the course and while he played, I would smack the golf ball up the fairway and chase after it. That's how I got started and before I knew it, I was competing in tournaments.

I grew up golfing at the Chanute Country Club. At the time, the golf pro was Kent Notestine, but everyone just called him Notey. He would later become a sort of second dad to me. I practiced more than anyone I knew. I hit bucket after bucket and putt after putt, sometimes until dark and even in the rain. I had one goal in mind and nothing was going to stop me from achieving it. That goal was to grow up and become a professional golfer.

I began entering junior events across Kansas. When I began winning those, my dad decided it was time to take my game to the next level. I started traveling to tournaments farther away and began competing at higher levels. As I continued to have success, Dad knew I had a special gift. When the time came, I decided to play college golf at Newman University where coincidentally, Notey would be my coach once again.

Despite the shortness of breath and weird heart beats, the first week of college was going great. When I arrived back in Wichita from my doctor's visit, I went straight to the golf course and began practicing. Qualifying was coming up and I needed my game to be in tip-top shape.

After I finished practicing, the guys and I decided to play 18 holes. When we finished playing, I noticed I was tired. Actually, I was more than tired. I was exhausted. About that time my phone started ringing. It was my mom.

"Hey son, I'm afraid I have some bad news," she said. "The doctor called and said that according to the chest x-ray, you have an enlarged heart. He wants you to go and see a specialist in Wichita. I scheduled you for Monday."

"Are you serious? Mom what's going to happen?" I asked in shock.

"Everything is going to be fine, Jeremy. Your dad and I will meet you in Wichita and we can go eat and go to the doctor," she said. I reminded her that qualifying was Monday and asked her to reschedule the appointment. She was worried about me playing in the heat of a normal Kansas summer, but I assured her I would be fine.

Mom got the appointment rescheduled for Tuesday and that Monday I qualified. I wasn't about to let a little heart problem stop me. This was my year and I was bound and determined to prove it.

Everything was going great, until the back nine came. That's when I began to notice severe fatigue along with a rapid heartbeat. It took everything I had to finish strong. I wouldn't admit it, but I knew something was wrong.

The next day my parents got to Wichita around noon. They picked me up and took me to a pizza place called Cici's Pizza (my favorite). We were also celebrating my dad's birthday which happened to fall on the same day. I loaded my plate with all different kinds of pizza and got a big side of ranch to dip it in, just like usual. We enjoyed our lunch together, then headed to the hospital.

When we arrived, I signed in and we sat down to wait.

"What do you think he's going to say?" I asked my parents.

"You're probably just going to get put on some medication and you'll be all lined out," Mom said.

"Well I hope you're right. And I hope they hurry up. I gotta get to golf practice," I said.

About that time I heard my name. As we were taken back to the exam room, a million thoughts were going through my head. Is there something wrong with my heart? Am I not running enough? Surely they will just put me on some pills for awhile.

We sat there waiting and wondering what was going to happen next. I was a little nervous, but more than anything just wanted to get back to the golf course. My game still needed some work before the next round of qualifying.

"Hey dad, how old are you again? 55? 60? It's hard to tell with that bald head of yours!" I said to him. I liked to give him a hard time every now and then, especially about his age and his baldness.

"You want an ass whoopin' boy?" he said sarcastically.

"I can take you any day, old man!" I said chuckling to him. About that time, there was a knock on the door.

"Hello, I'm Dr. Lloyd. How are you guys today?" the doctor said. "You're probably ready to get to the golf course, so let me tell you what we're going to be doing today. Basically we need to take a look at your heart in a more detailed manner to see exactly what is going on. To do this, you need to have an echocardiogram. You have nothing to worry about. This is simply a machine we use that gives us all the information we need to know. All you have to do is take your shirt off and lay down on a table. Then the tech will perform your echo. Any questions?"

"Nope. I'm just ready to get it over with!" I said.

This didn't seem that bad at all. I figured I'd have to go through a lot of tests but this was nothing.

Dr. Lloyd led us to the echo room where we met the tech and got situated. He then explained the procedure.

"There is nothing to it. I will put this gel-like substance on a probe and look at your heart from all different angles."

My parents were in the room with us and as we watched the screen, the tech explained what we saw.

"This is the left ventricle and this is your mitral valve," he said to us.

"Wow, that's really cool," I said.

"Did you know you had a bicuspid valve?" he asked me.

"No, I have never been told that," I said.

"Well it's not that uncommon; a lot of people have this. All it means is that you have two leaflets instead of three in your valve. Here, can you see the two leaflets where I'm pointing?" he asked me.

"Yeah, that's wild. I never knew that," I told him.

He went about his business but as he progressed, he was less talkative until he eventually stopped talking altogether. At the time I didn't think much of it, but I did hear my dad whisper to my mom, "Why did he stop talking? This isn't good."

"Well, we're all done. You did great! Why don't you guys go ahead and have a seat back in your room and Dr. Lloyd and I will take a look at the results and do some calculations. When we're done, we'll come in and let you know what we found," he said to us.

"Well that was easy," I said to my parents.

"Yeah, it was cool how they did that. So are you going to go golf now?" Mom asked.

"Yup, I gotta get practiced up. We have our second round of qualifying coming up," I said.

"Well that'll be fun. I'm glad we got to see you today. When do you think you'll be home next?" they asked me.

About that time the door opened and Dr. Lloyd came in and sat down. He said to us, "Hey guys, sorry about the wait. We do have your results back. Unfortunately, they aren't so good. Your ejection fraction is severely low and your mitral and atrial valves are leaking blood back into your lungs. This explains why you are having trouble breathing. We are going to have to admit you immediately into the hospital. I'm afraid this is going to be much more than just getting put on some medicine. We need to do several tests on you to determine if your valves can be repaired. One thing is for sure. Your life is going to change drastically from here on out."

"For I know the plans I have for you,"

declares the LORD, "plans to prosper

you and not to harm you, plans to

give you hope and a future."

Jeremiah 29:11

Chapter Two

Heartbreak

I was in utter shock. I didn't know what to think. They must have messed up the echo or switched some numbers up. I mean look at me! I can't be having heart problems. I have school and golf to worry about; I can't afford this.

"Now if you will just follow me, we will get you on your way," Dr. Lloyd said.

When we got to the admission room, all of us were in shock. No one had a clue what was going on. From there I was put in a hospital gown and wheeled out to my room where I would be spending most of my time the next few days. I will say this: the hospital was a very nice place. I was impressed. But I didn't belong there. I belonged anywhere but there.

As I was lying in bed wondering what was going to happen to me next, I heard mom on her phone.

"Dad," Mom said.

"Yes, Lisa?" Grandpa said.

"You need to get here as soon as you can. Things aren't good," Mom said.

"Oh dear....okay we're on our way," Grandpa said.

Whenever something was wrong, it seems like not only are my parents always there, but my grandparents as well. We are all very close and I missed them dearly at this point. For some reason, when I'm around all of them, I feel like everything is going to be okay. I needed that now more than ever.

As we got situated in our room, Mom and Dad began calling everyone to let them know the news. Meanwhile, I was being hooked up to the machines and having IVs started and needles jabbed in me. This was only the beginning of what I would go through.

The doctors came in after a while and told us that I would be monitored for tonight and that first thing tomorrow, I would have a heart cath done which would assure us of what we needed to do. Dr. Khicha, the surgeon, would visit with us after he looked over the results of the cath and let us know where to go from there.

"So you don't think he will have to have any sort of transplantation or anything like that do you?" Mom said.

"I highly doubt that. Judging from what we've seen, I think it's just going to be a valve replacement, but we always have to be sure. The heart cath will tell us everything we need to know. If the valve replacement cannot get your ejection fraction back to the level it needs to be then yes, you will be looking at a heart transplant," Doc said.

"Okay, thank you doctor," Mom said.

"Well at least he didn't think a transplant would be necessary. That gives me a little relief. I don't know what I would do if I had to go through that. This is bad enough," I said to Mom.

"You'll be fine son. Just try and get some rest for tomorrow. We have a big day ahead of us," Mom said.

"I'm gonna go get a hotel and go to bed. Mom will stay here with you tonight. You'll be fine, my boy," Dad said.

As I lay in bed that first night at the hospital, a million thoughts were going through my head. What would I do with school? What about golf? Am I going to die? At 19 years old? Surely not! Sleep that night was pretty much nonexistent.

Well, let's face it, despite all of the thoughts storming around in my head, sleeping in a hospital is pretty much impossible anyway. There's always so much beeping, people coughing, an uncomfortable bed, and that dreadful hospital smell. Oh well, I thought, tomorrow will be here before I know it.

When I awoke the next day, my cath was first thing in the morning. I couldn't eat or drink anything after midnight so I was absolutely starving. The nurse came in to instruct me on what was going to happen and told me I needed to take off all my clothes and put on this robe (or I could wear my boxers if I felt uncomfortable). Being that I was going to be around my family, I felt better wearing my boxers under the robe. But there was one problem. I didn't know I was going to be admitted into the hospital so I was completely unprepared. I was still wearing my underwear from the day before which were quite hilarious. They were American Eagle boxers which had bananas all over them and read "big banana."

"Oh my gosh," I thought. "The nurses and doctors are going to get a kick out of this."

As I was being wheeled into the holding room, I said goodbye to my parents and began my journey of testing. I was lying on this bed in a corner of the room as the doctors and nurses were preparing their things and I couldn't help but notice the window beside me. It was a beautiful day out and I wished dearly that I could be outside playing golf or doing anything for that matter. Anything but lying in the hospital.

"Jeremy, we have to numb the back of your throat so we can insert this camera down it during the test. I need you to open your mouth and I will spray this banana tasting substance on your throat. It will probably burn and sting for awhile but it will eventually get numb and go away," the nurse said.

You know, despite being in a hospital, I really couldn't help but laugh on the inside. I'm wearing big banana boxers and I get to be numbed by a banana tasting substance. What a coincidence. I wish I could hear what the doctors and nurses said about that.

Once she sprayed the substance, it did burn pretty badly and it was a really awkward feeling. Once it went away though, it felt like my entire mouth had no feeling at all. It was one of the weirdest things I have ever felt. Honestly, I had no idea what kind of testing they were going to do. I just knew they were going to do a heart cath and go in to look and see exactly what the problem was. Besides that, I was just going with it. After the spray they would inject some medicine in my IV that would relax me until I fell asleep. The last thing I remember is some doctors talking and being wheeled into some room. Then I was out.

As I awoke, I remember this extreme pain around my groin. That is where they went in for the heart cath. When the nurses found out I had awakened, they came into my room and told me to keep lying flat and they would let me know when I could get up. "Damn!" I thought, "This hurts like hell!" Any of you reading this who have had a heart cath know it's not fun, especially when they go in through the groin. When I was finally able to get out of bed and walk around, it hurt even worse. I was limping around the room like I had been shot in the leg. On top of this, I had to pee like a Russian racehorse! As I stood there in the bathroom, I remember waiting and waiting and waiting and nothing seemed to be close to coming out. Finally it began to start hurting to the point that I couldn't take it anymore. For some reason, having a cath in the groin was not allowing me to pee. I pushed my call button and told the nurse that I was going to need them to put a catheter in me or I was going to explode. I hated to do this, as I had heard some stories about catheters, but I had no other choice.

Normally when people get catheters they are asleep; they get them during surgery. The only thing most people have to worry about is having them pulled out. I, on the other hand, well I wasn't so lucky. I had to be wide awake. Unfortunately, it was a male nurse who walked in my room with the supplies. It might have been a little better if a supermodel in a nurse outfit put it in, but, oh well.

As I pulled my pants down and got situated, the only thing that was going through my mind was, "Please let's get this over with. This is so freaking awkward." The nurse assured me I had nothing to worry about and it would burn for a few seconds but once it got into my bladder I would feel much better. When I saw the size of the tube he was about to insert you know where, I about shit myself. "There is no way that thing is going in me!" I thought.

"Take a deep breath and hold it," the nurse said.

A piercing pain went through me. I gritted my teeth and tried not to kick him in the face. Once the tube got all the way to my bladder, I did start to feel relieved, but it was still such an awkward feeling. I would definitely have to get used to this.

Once that was finally over, I had the rest of the day to relax in bed and await the test results, which I would know first thing in the morning. Later on that day, some family and friends started to arrive to keep me and my parents company. You can imagine how shocked everyone was when they found out the news. I was the last person anyone would think this would happen to. It was also amazing to see just how many people cared about me. Almost all of my family and friends were there to support me including my golf coach and even the president of Newman University. I needed their support now more than ever, as tomorrow would be a life-changing day. That night when I was ready for bed, Dad went to the hotel with Grandma and Grandpa. Mom stayed with me at the hospital.

That next morning at 7 a.m. sharp, Dr. Khicha came in to inform us of the results of the testing.

"How are you guys this morning?" he said.

"Tired," we all agreed.

"Well, I'm going to get right to the point. Your heart is functioning at 10 percent. After reviewing your file and testing, even if they replaced your valves, I don't feel like I could buy you more than a year's time. Your heart is so far gone that if we did a valve replacement, your ejection fraction probably wouldn't get up to where it needed to be. I'm sorry Mr. Gant, but I'm going to recommend you for a heart transplant as soon as possible," he said.

At that moment my mom and I just kind of looked at each other in total shock. We didn't know what to say or how to act.

"I will give you some time. Dr. Lloyd and Dr. Estep will be in shortly to talk to you about the transplant process," he said.

When Dr. Khicha left the room, I completely lost it. Words cannot describe the feelings that went through me at that time. It was as if someone had punched you right in the stomach as hard as they could. Mom immediately got on the phone and called Dad and Grandma and Grandpa. They were still at the hotel as it was only around 7:30 a.m. When they arrived we all were in tears and just tried to give each other some comfort. None of us saw this coming. A heart transplant was the last thing we would ever have expected. As I lay there with my family in tears, I was praying that this all was a dream. "I have to wake up sometime," I thought, "This can't be real."

There was a knock on the door and in came Dr. Estep and Dr. Lloyd. They first expressed their sympathy, but at the same time they assured me that everything was going to be fine. My family and I were still in shock about the whole deal and we let the doctors do the talking. At this point there was nothing we could really do but listen. They went on about the whole transplant process and getting on the list and basically gave us a broad outlook of what was about to happen in our near future.

"So all this will be done here right?" I asked the doctors.

"Unfortunately we do not do transplants here anymore. You will be flown to St. Luke's in Kansas City where they will take care of the rest of the process. I assure you, they are very good at what they do. We are contacting them now and getting everything set up. I believe you will be flown there by helicopter in a few hours," Dr. Lloyd said.

When they left, we all sat in the room waiting for what was going to happen next.

"God," I said to my family, "as soon as you think you've heard it all."

"Everything's going to be okay, honey. It does stink that they can't do everything here, but I'm sure Kansas City is very good. We're going to get through this," Mom said.

About that time, more people started showing up, including my teammates. My girlfriend was there as well. They all provided me with some comfort for the time being. They all took turns coming into my room and visiting me and trying to assure me I was going to be okay.

After a couple of hours, a nurse came in and said, "There is bad weather around Kansas City so they are going to fly you by airplane instead of by helicopter. You will be ambulanced to the airport and then leave for St. Luke's. They will be in to get you shortly."

I started to say my goodbyes to everyone, even though it seemed like they had just gotten there. Before long I was being strapped down to be transported.

I'll never forget when the paramedics were pushing me out of the hospital toward the ambulance. All of my family and friends were lined up to tell me goodbye and that they loved me. People I would have never thought cared about me so much were there with tears running down their faces. I was so scared, yet I knew I had to be brave. I waved at everyone and told them I loved them and I would see them soon. My mom would be riding with me on the airplane and my dad would drive back to Chanute to get our things and then head to Kansas City the next day. As the last person faded from sight, I knew that my journey to a new life had just begun.

Despite everything that was going on, I was a little disappointed that we were riding in an airplane instead of a helicopter. I had ridden on many airplanes before but never a helicopter. But I had bigger things to worry about than how I got to fly. As the ambulance pulled up to the airport and I was being wheeled onto the plane, I could see a line of cars and people in the distance waving goodbye to me. They had driven to the airport to see me one last time and watch me fly away in the distance. "How blessed I am," I thought, "to have such wonderful people surrounding me."

It was a mess to try and get me situated on this tiny plane with all my cords and wires dangling everywhere. Once I was positioned and they had me in a comfortable place, we got ready for takeoff. I loved flying in planes so this was perhaps the most enjoyment I had gotten out of this whole ordeal. Plus it was nearing darkness so we were able to see the sun go down from the plane and all the lights from the different cities and towns.

When we arrived in Kansas City, there was an ambulance waiting at the airport to take me to the hospital. It was completely dark out when we arrived at the hospital and from what I could see, we pulled into what looked like a small garage. They wheeled my bed, which I was still strapped to, out of the ambulance and onto the elevator where we would proceed upward to get checked in.

When we exited the elevator, we had to go through the ER/ Trauma center in order to get to admissions. This was the last thing I expected and man was it a nightmare. There were people screaming and crying and doctors running around and to me it just looked like a whole bunch of chaos.

At the admission desk, they put a new bracelet on my wrist and went through the whole information process that I'm sure a lot of you are familiar with. Not the most fun thing in the world I can tell you that. Especially not late at night. Once that was over, they put me in a room and told me that my nurse would be in shortly. I could see the tears start to run down my mom's face. Once again I knew I had to be strong not only for myself but for my family as well.

At the time I wasn't feeling very well and was running a fever. Once the nurse started going over everything, I could tell I wasn't going to like him. I was freezing and extremely thirsty and this hard-ass seemed to think all I could have was a cup of ice. As far as blankets go, I got only a thin sheet to lie under because according to him, "I needed to shiver my fever away."

"Okay," I thought, "All this makes *perfect* sense. I'm on my deathbed and all you can do is make things even more miserable for me. I thought a nurse's job was to make the patient feel as calm and collected as possible. Sure, maybe these are techniques to healing a fever but you don't use them on a 19-year old who can snap you like a twig and is on the verge of a mental breakdown."

It got worse though. My chances of getting any sleep that night were ruined.

"We need to put these cuffs on each of your legs to keep your blood circulating. They will squeeze and un-squeeze each of your legs throughout the night," my nurse said.

I just about punched him square in the face. "Really? Is this necessary?" I thought, "My dinkus is already hibernating for the winter and now I have to deal with this all night?"

In addition to the cords hooked up to me and the cuffs on my leg, the room was brighter than all get out and the hospital bed was like lying on a cement floor. There were constant beeping noises and nurses were in every few hours to take my temperature and draw blood. Instead of sleeping, I simply sat up in my bed and began my long journey of praying to God that this would all be over soon. In between praying, I would get on my phone and listen to music to try and relax myself. I would occasionally doze off for a few minutes but that was about it. I had a long night ahead of me. Tomorrow would mark the first day of the evaluation process.

"Even though I walk through the valley of the shadow of death, I fear no evil, for You are with me; Your rod and Your staff, they comfort me."

Psalm 23:4

Chapter Three

Evaluation

I awoke the next morning to a needle being shoved into my arm. It was that time of the morning where the lab people go around and draw blood. I never did understand why they had to do it so early in the morning but that's beside the point. After they left, I fell back asleep until my breakfast came.

A little while after finishing breakfast, my dad arrived. It was a bittersweet moment because as happy as we were to see him, he walked in as I was lying in bed getting ready to experience more pain than I could ever imagine.

"How are you doing son?" Dad said.

"I'm doing okay, I guess. Just ready to see what they have to say. Last night was terrible, I didn't get any sleep at all," I said.

About that time, one of the main nurse coordinators came in and introduced herself. We had been waiting most of the morning for her visit, as she was the one who would tell us what was going to happen in these many weeks to come.

"Hello Jeremy, how are you?" she said.

"I've been better," I said.

"I bet you have. Well listen, I'm sorry to hear about your situation. It's tough to go through this at such a young age. I promise you though, we are going to get you a good young heart and you'll be out of here in no time. Sound good?" she said.

"Sounds great," I replied.

She went on to tell us about the whole evaluation process, but first she asked for our insurance information. A heart transplant costs a lot of money. If your insurance doesn't approve it, you're out of luck. Fortunate enough for us, we had good insurance and would be approved a few days later.

The coordinator began to brief us on everything that was going to happen in the coming months. The whole point of the evaluation was to make sure I didn't have any serious health problems that might limit the success of my transplant. Over the next few weeks, I would be put through many different tests and be visited by every kind of doctor imaginable. I had to be looked at from head to toe to make sure I didn't have a condition that might affect the transplant. If one single thing was wrong, even with my teeth or my feet, it had to be corrected immediately. If it couldn't be, it could mean no transplant. It was one of the hardest things I've ever had to deal with. The pain both physically and mentally never seemed to end.

I had to be seen by a psychiatrist so my emotional state and support system could be discussed and monitored. When one goes through all these tests, a psychiatrist is always good to have on hand because it can be a very grueling process to go through. The psychiatrist talked to me about my past and how I felt about everything that was going to happen and if I had any concerns. Basically it was her job to make sure I was as calm as I could possibly be. If I was stressed or in an emotionally damaged state, I was recommended to talk to the psychiatrist. I was okay with this starting off, but as the weeks passed I began to have my doubts, which I will discuss later on.

A lung doctor visited me during the evaluation process as well. He would examine my lungs and make sure there was nothing wrong with them as one has to have healthy lungs for a heart to function properly. The doctors always need to know if you smoke because bad lungs can lead to a lot of problems down the road.

I was to see my dentist, who was in Chanute, to make sure there were no infections in my gums or teeth. This may not sound like a big deal, but if there is a problem or an infection, it can travel straight to the heart which can lead to complications in the transplant process. There have been some instances where all of a patient's teeth had to be pulled before transplant. I knew I had perfect teeth, as I visited the dentist regularly, but it was interesting to know this for future reference.

The next set of doctors I remember very well, as there were many of them and they came in to see me quite often. These were the infectious disease doctors, whose job was to make sure I hadn't had any bad infections or diseases in my past that might cause complications during transplant. They asked me questions dating all the way back to when I was a baby. If I had the chicken pox, they had to know when. If I had the flu, same thing. I admire them because their job would be quite strenuous. If they overlooked one small thing, it could cost me my life.

I was very lucky I was in good shape; otherwise, I would have to be examined by another long list of physicians. For instance, if I was a diabetic I would have to see an eye doctor and an endocrinologist to make sure I didn't have any advanced cases of diabetes that would affect the transplant. If I had problems with my stomach or bowels, I would have to see a gastroenterologist to have that checked out. If I had kidney problems, I would have to see a nephrologist or kidney specialist to have all that checked out. The list goes on and on. You can see how this process could take a very long time if one was not healthy. These were just the specialists I had to see, but I haven't mentioned all the fellows and other regular doctors that visited me on a daily basis. There was always something going on in my room. By the time night came, I was exhausted.

Now that I've mentioned all the doctors that came to see me, we can move on to the hard part of the process. Test after test after test. I would see a doctor and then get prepped for a test. When I woke up, I would see another doctor and have another test. Like I said, it was one of the hardest things I have ever had to go through, and I hadn't even had the transplant yet.

Let's begin with the blood draws. Several tubes of blood were drawn to test all sorts of things such as blood type, tissue type, hepatitis, kidney function, liver function, syphilis, AIDS, and chickenpox to name a few. They did this so frequently that I actually learned to sleep through the blood draws. I would sleep with my arm out and they would go about their business and I would continue sleeping. I'll tell you this: if you're scared of needles, you're going to have a hell of a time getting a heart transplant.

If I hadn't had a flu shot or pneumonia vaccination in the past six years, I had to be given those. Fortunately, I had received those prior to evaluation. Two skin tests were done, one on each arm, to test for tuberculosis and mumps. These were checked a day or two after having received them in order to monitor the results. A pulmonary function test was done which measured my lung capacity. This test was actually kind of cool since there was no pain involved. I remember sitting on a crazy looking machine with some sort of mask on and doing various breathing exercises. I rode on a bike and performed a few other small tests as well.

The 24-hour urine test was quite entertaining because I had to save each urine specimen in the container I was given. If I chose to pee somewhere else in the hospital, the test had to be started over. As you all probably know, this was another test which measured my kidney function. I don't know about you, but having to do a urine and bowel specimen wasn't my favorite thing in the world. I felt so bad for the nurses that had to collect them. I guess that's their job though.

The next step was for me to be sent to the radiology department for numerous x-rays on my chest and jaw. Once these were done, I had to have an abdominal sonogram to look at my gallbladder, kidneys, liver, and abdominal aorta. A CT scan wasn't necessary since I didn't smoke in the past.

I had to go to the vascular laboratory to have a sound wave test that measured the flow of blood in the arteries in my neck and legs. These tests are often called carotid duplex and peripheral vascular Doppler studies. I had to have some tests of my GI tract done by the gastroenterologists. For those tests I was required to not eat for half a day in order for the doctors to get a good picture of my GI tract. This was hard for me because I love to eat, but being that I was in the hospital eating that food and not a pizza, I was okay with it. Are you getting a better picture of the process? Not much fun for a 19 year-old guy.

An EKG and echocardiogram were the next tests, which were no big deal. Basically they hook up tons of wires to you and get a detailed picture of the heart's beats. This makes sure the heart isn't out of rhythm or anything like that. I'm sure a lot of you have had one of these done and you know they're not a big deal, just another pain-in-the-ass test. I do have a history with the echo, if you remember, so in a way I enjoyed it and it reminded me of how this all got started.

The next test was a different story. I had to have a right heart catheterization as well as a heart biopsy performed at the same time. Not the most fun thing in the world I'll tell you that, especially since I just had it done in Wichita. A lot of these tests I've mentioned having to do with my heart were performed in Wichita, but they wanted to do them again to make sure the first tests were right and compare the results. For them it was "better safe than sorry," but for me it just meant more pain. The purpose of these tests was to measure the pressure in the right side of my heart, as well as to see if I had any inflammation of the heart muscle. These tests required that I be put out or "relaxed" as they stuck long tubes down me and whatever else they did. I know I sure as hell didn't want to be awake during any of this.

I have had a few of these caths done so I can tell you a bit about them. They prep you and put you in a holding room with a bunch of other people who are waiting to have the same thing done (or something similar). There's always a bunch of hacking and coughing going on and it's just not a fun place to be. Once your name is called, a nurse comes and gets you and wheels you into the operating room. It's always freezing in the op room and I hate it. The first thing I say is, "Can I please get some warm blankets?" They strap you onto the operating table, which is like a freaking two by four. It's extremely small and uncomfortable. At that point you just wait for the "relaxing" medicine. The doctors come in and talk and joke around until it's time to administer the medicine. Once the medicine hits you, you don't remember much. Sometimes, I could feel the wire moving through me, which is a little weird but other than that you usually wake up in the recovery room not knowing what happened and you just feel tired as hell.

During all of these tests, it is the nurse coordinator's job to inform you of the results. Every once in a while the doctor who performed the test will come in and tell you about it as well. When all of the tests are completed, the transplant team gathers and makes a decision as to whether you are suitable for transplant or not. This isn't an easy decision and usually takes a little bit of time as each patient is evaluated individually. Once the decision is made, however, the nurse coordinator or one of the cardiologists will come into your room and inform you of the final decision.

It's funny how God works. If it wasn't for two events happening during all of the testing, I don't think I could have made it through everything. The first event was simply a phone call I received. Months before I knew I needed a heart transplant, I was watching The Golf Channel and saw a special about a guy named Erik Compton. He was a PGA Tour golfer who had just received his second heart transplant. I thought it was pretty crazy how he was able to compete on the PGA after having gone through not one but two heart transplants. I never forgot about Erik's story. Low and behold, a few months later I would be sitting in a hospital waiting to see if I would get to receive a heart transplant. It just so happened that my parents had gotten in contact with his mom who then told Erik about my story.

One day as I was lying in bed resting from all the tests, my dad came marching through the door and said in an excited tone, "Jeremy, there's an Erik Compton on the phone? He wants to talk to you."

"What???" I yelled.

He handed me the phone and with a huge smile on my face I answered, "Hello?"

"Hey Jeremy, this is Erik Compton. How are you?" Erik said.

"Well a lot better now, man! What's going on?" I said.

"I heard you were being evaluated for a heart transplant and just wanted to see how you were doing and if you had any questions," Erik said.

For the next hour, Erik and I talked about everything from heart transplants to golf. Hell, we even shot the shit about women. He knew I was scared only being 19, so when I had a question he would answer it accordingly and assure me everything was going to be fine. This was quite a unique conversation because he's one of the only people that I could have that conversation with. I can't ask my best friend or my college professor what it feels like to be on anti-rejection medicine or what it feels like to wake up after undergoing a heart transplant because they've never experienced it. Erik, on the other hand, I could ask anything because he'd already been on the path I was about to experience. He'd been there not just once but twice.

As the conversation came to an end, I remember the last thing I asked him. It was a very simple question but it had been on my mind ever since I found out I needed a new heart.

"Erik," I said, "Will I ever have my life back again?"

He said calmly, "Well, I just got done playing 18 holes and now I'm headed back home to see my wife and kids. If that's not a life, then I don't know what is."

As tears began to roll down my face, I replied, "Thanks man, you're the best."

Erik told me that if I ever needed anything to just give him a call and he'd be glad to help. To this day we still talk quite often and continue to give each other support.

The second event took place a few days after Erik's phone call. I was still ecstatic about the phone call and just when I thought things couldn't get any better, they did. As I was lying in bed one afternoon watching TV, there came a knock on the door.

"Is this Jeremy Gant's room?" a voice said.

"Yeah, come on in!" I said in a tired tone.

About that time my dad nudged me and said, "Jeremy, sit up sit up!"

"Hello, I'm Tom Watson and this is my wife Hilary. How are you doing, Jeremy?" Watson said.

I was in complete and utter disbelief. Tom Watson, one of the greatest golfers to ever play the game, had just walked into my room and started having a conversation with me like we'd known each other all our lives. My parents and grandparents were in my room as well and they were in just as much shock as I was. We watched him on TV all the time and here he was!

Once I gathered myself, I shakily replied, "I'm pretty good. I can't believe you're here! This is crazy! "

"Naw, I'm just a normal person like you. I heard from Tod Palmer that a college golfer he knew was in the hospital needing a heart transplant so I figured I'd come pay you a visit. How are things going?" Watson said.

Tod used to be a sports writer for the Chanute Tribune. When I was growing up, he wrote all of my golf articles. In fact, he wrote my very first article.

"Right now is tough because I have to undergo a lot of testing and it's not very fun. But today is going a lot better now that you're here!" I said with a smile on my face.

It was quite amazing how down-to-earth Tom was. Here was a guy who was known around the world as one of the best golfers to ever play the game and he still took the time out of his busy schedule to come to the hospital and see someone he didn't even know. If that doesn't tell you anything about what a good guy Watson is, I don't know what will.

He and his wife sat and talked to us in that tiny hospital room for more than an hour about all kinds of things. It seemed like we had known Tom our whole lives. I'd be talking to Tom about golf and my parents would be talking to Hilary about horses and then my grandparents would chime in and mention how they watch Tom all the time on TV. It seemed like something out of a dream and I made sure to cherish every second of it.

It was funny because during our conversation Tom asked me a sort of trick question. "Speaking of golf, who is your favorite golfer?" Tom said with a grin on his face. Without even thinking I replied, "Tiger Woods!" As soon as I said it I turned bright red and thought, "You idiot!" It was fine though because Tom immediately winked at me and began showering Tiger with compliments. Right before Tom and Hilary left, we got some pictures of all of us together. Then Tom took off his hat and autographed it and also gave me a signed copy of his DVD, *Lessons of a Lifetime*. "This guy is truly unbelievable," I thought.

"It was a pleasure meeting you Jeremy and I wish you the best of luck. You will be in our prayers and I will continue to stay updated on your progress," Tom said as he was leaving the room.

With tears in my eyes I responded, "Thanks again for everything, Tom. You are truly amazing. I'll be watching you on TV! See you guys!"

As he left, we were all kind of quiet for a moment. I was still in shock from Erik's call. Tom Watson walking through the door a few days later left me speechless.

"He was such an amazing guy," I said to my family, "and Hilary is really sweet as well."

"Yes, they are both truly a blessing from God. It's amazing how He works," my mom said.

"Yes, yes it is," I said.

Once everything had calmed down and the testing was finally over, I was extremely tired and anxious at the same time. I couldn't sleep because I wanted to hear what the doctor's decision was going to be. If I didn't qualify for a transplant, my life would be over. They gave me less than a year to live without it. Hell, even if I *did* qualify for a transplant, I still had to go through that process, and it wasn't a perfect guarantee.

I still don't know how it happened but that night my life changed forever. It was Dad's turn to stay with me; Mom would be staying with our relatives. They usually took turns staying with me because the rooms only had one little chair unless we were lucky enough to get a small, portable bed. I was physically and emotionally drained from all the testing and evaluations. I was at that point where reality was starting to hit me and I just didn't know if I could do it anymore. "Why is this happening to me?" I thought. "I could really die and I'm only 19."

Sleeping that night was impossible, so something inside me decided to pop in *The Passion of the Christ*. I figured I would get tired and fall asleep, but as the movie kept going, I seemed to somehow relive what was going on. I could feel the pain of Jesus getting whipped and Him carrying the cross and being crucified. As the tears started to roll down my face, I could feel the whips hitting my back and the nails being driven into my hands. Each scene made me realize the journey I was being taken on was nothing compared to His.

Suddenly the pain inside me seemed to cease. If He can go through all of that for us, then surely I can get through this. And from that night on everything seemed to get a lot easier for me. Sure, I would still get scared at times, but there was always that voice inside of me that said everything would be alright. Somehow all of the prayers that had been sent up to Him on my behalf had been answered. It was as if He just came to me and put His hand on my shoulder and said, "Everything is going to be okay. It's all part of the plan." And a plan it would be.

The next morning, I had just woken up and eaten breakfast and was watching ESPN on the tiny TV that was in our room. I heard a knock on the door and the nurse coordinator and one of my doctors came in. I quickly turned off the TV and gave her my complete attention. She asked how my morning was going and then got straight down to business.

"Jeremy, we have all the test results back and I'm pleased to tell you that you have been approved for a heart transplant and have been put on the list as a status 1B," she said.

I didn't have much to say. I was so happy and thankful that all of my prayers had been answered. All I could manage was an, "Oh my gosh, that's awesome."

Once I got over the exciting news, she began to tell me more about what was to come. First off, she told me what a status 1B actually meant. There are four statuses that a transplant patient on the list can be classified under. These are status 1A, status 1B, status 2, or status 7. Status 1A patients are the highest priority as they are the ones who are severely sick and have to wait in the hospital to receive a heart. Normally they are on some sort of LVAD or some form of a life-support machine. Since I caught my problem early, I was healthy enough that I didn't quite need an LVAD or any form of life-support, so I was put on the second priority list, which is Status 1B. These patients are connected to an intravenous medicine such as Primacor that feeds through an IV in order to keep you alive. 1B patients can either wait in a hospital or wait at home, depending on their condition. Status 2 patients are not connected to any life support devices or intravenous feeds and see the cardiologist on a regular basis. Status 2 patients usually wait the longest to receive a transplant, if they receive one at all. If the patient gets sick, however, they can always move up in status on the list. Status 7 patients are temporarily inactive, which can be caused by a number of reasons. They will accrue time on the list but are unavailable for a transplant.

After I heard all this, I realized that I had gotten extremely lucky. A Status 1B is the perfect spot to be in because you're sick but not too sick, and you don't have to stay in the hospital if they pass you to go home. At the time, I didn't quite know what an intravenous feed was or how it worked, but I figured it was no big deal. "Maybe this won't be so bad after all," I thought. Boy, was I wrong!

"But the day of the Lord will come like a thief, in which the heavens will pass away with a roar and the elements will be destroyed with intense heat..."

2 Peter 3:10

Chapter Four

Waiting...

As the day went on, I was getting more and more anxious to come home. It had been a while and judging by the way my nurse talked, I would get to wait at home for a heart. Come to find out, Labor Day weekend was approaching and this meant that more than likely there would be some accidents on the road from all the travelers. It was bittersweet to think about but my chances of getting a heart went up drastically this weekend. As a result, the doctors wanted to keep me in the hospital over the weekend just in case this did happen. That way they could continue to monitor my heart and make sure all the choices they had made thus far were the right ones.

I wasn't too happy about this, but the sooner I could get this whole transplant thing over with the better. I would much rather be in a hospital when I got the call than at home doing who-knows-what and having to drive back to KC. Maybe I could get lucky; if not, I was still accruing time on the list so it was a win-win situation. Plus, as much as I hate hospitals, there is this part of me that likes them because you know that if something happens to you, you're always going to be safe.

That weekend at the hospital was a crazy one to say the least. I was a very well-known kid in my hometown and in

Wichita. With everything happening so fast and me going from Wichita to KC, there were a lot of people still freaking out who wanted to see me. I had more than 70 people at St. Luke's that weekend who came to see me. It got to the point where I had to turn people away because I would get so overwhelmed and tired. I was still going through a few tests every day, so I was just exhausted.

It was nice to see all these people who cared about me so much, though. There were people who came to see me that I wouldn't have predicted in a million years to be there. They brought gifts and games and movies and all kinds of things just to help keep me occupied during my stay. One thing that I enjoyed was seeing all these people coming together. It truly touched my heart and helped me make it through everything.

There was something else that went on that weekend that helped me immensely in my journey. A 21 year-old girl by the name of Kayla had just gotten a heart transplant and was a few days post-surgery. She only had to wait six days on her heart, which was incredibly quick. As I was doing my daily laps around the rooms, I noticed she happened to be on the same floor as I was. "Man," I thought, "a person close to my age who had a heart transplant. If I could somehow talk to her, that would be really special."

Later in the day, one of my nurses was doing her rounds and when she knocked on the door I asked her to come to me for a second.

"Hey, you know that girl Kayla?" I asked, "Do you think that I could meet her and ask her some questions sometime before she leaves?"

"Well of course you can! I'll stop by and talk to her later and ask her if she would stop by and see you," she said.

Later in the weekend, I was laying in bed talking to my parents when I heard a knock on the door. "You have a visitor!" my nurse said. About that time I saw a young girl wearing a hospital gown and a mask step into the room.

"Hey, I'm Kayla! How are you?" she said.

I was in total awe and could only muster out an, "I'm good!" I had never seen a heart transplant patient before and here was one close to my age, a few days out, just standing next to me. I had so many questions to ask her but at the same time I knew she was probably exhausted and in a lot of pain. I tried to make it brief.

"Wow, you look great! How does it feel?" I said.

"It takes some getting used to but each day gets a lot better. I can already begin to tell the difference. You can kind of see my scar," she said.

Her being a girl I could only see half the scar, but it still looked really good. It was hard to believe that this was going to be me sometime soon. At least I hoped.

We kept talking and her dad was with her so eventually my parents and her dad went out to the lobby and talked so she and I could have some one-on-one time to talk. This was good because her dad had been through the whole process and could relate that back to my parents which would help them out a lot. Plus there's only one person that can relate to and help a heart transplant patient and that's another person who's had the same thing done to them. That is why talking to Kayla was so important to me.

Kayla and I talked for a bit until she started to get tired. She told me about waiting and about the surgery and what all goes on. I asked the occasional question like, "What does it feel like when you wake up," or "What does a biopsy feel like?" She would calmly answer me and assure me that it was going to be scary at first, but everything would be fine. They told her that each person takes it differently and has their own problems. For instance, she said that she had problems with the biopsy and that she had another issue that was a whole other surgery. This aside, it was just a really cool experience to have a patient who's been through the same thing you're about to go through sit down and touch base with you emotionally and assure you everything will be okay.

Once she left, my parents came back in and shared their experience with me and told me how much it had helped them to talk to someone who had gone through what they were about to go through. I know my side of the situation is tough but I can't imagine what it would be like for my parents. Having a kid that is doing great in life and then all of a sudden is told he has less than a year to live. Having to sleep in a hospital chair by their son every night, praying that he gets a heart before he dies. That's unbelievable to think about and makes my respect and love for my parents grow more and more each time I think about it.

Once the weekend passed and Labor Day had come and gone, I came to the realization that I was probably going to have to go home and wait on my heart. The average waiting time for St. Luke's is around 30 days anyway, so it wasn't a big deal. I knew this would probably happen but there is always that small chance.

Sure enough, one of my doctors came in and informed me that I was going to be sent home but I would need to have a few things done before that would happen. First off, I would have to have a PICC line put in my arm or an intravenous feed as mentioned earlier. Since I was a status 1B, I had to have this done in order to keep my heart pumping. What I didn't realize at the time is that my heart could literally fail at any moment. This was a way to buy me more time.

Getting the PICC line put in was a small surgery in itself and required trained nurses to do so. Once I found out there would be a long tube in me and I would have to carry around a portable IV pump, I began to get a little nervous. Suddenly going home seemed a lot worse than I had thought it would be. Nevertheless, I knew God wouldn't let anything happen to me. I gritted my teeth and tried to enjoy the whole process. I was going to be home-free pretty soon, so the faster I got this over with, the better.

It turned out to be no big deal at all. My nurse was a nice old gal and reminded me a lot of my grandmother. You could tell she had done this a million times, which made me feel at ease. Before I knew it, the line was in and the procedure was all done. What I thought was going to be painful was nothing at all. Having this line in my arm would take some getting used to, but I hoped and prayed it wouldn't be for long.

The next step would be a big decision in which I had only partial say in the matter. In order to go home, you have to have a defibrillator "installed" in you. Now normally, this is a whole other surgery that would require more time in the hospital and a lot more pain. Luckily there was another option. They had just released what they called a LifeVest in which you could actually wear a vest-like gadget containing the defibrillator and then put your shirt over that. It wouldn't be the most comfortable thing but it would mean no surgery. When the doctors asked me about which option I like best, I immediately told them the external defibrillator. If I could avoid another surgery, I was all for it. The only problem was that they had to approve me for this option. Usually people have been so sick in the past that they either already have a defibrillator installed or they just elect for one, so this option was quite new. The doctors told me they were going to get together and discuss what would be best for me and then let me know. Meanwhile I was told to wait, which was a term I was getting quite used to hearing.

The next day, a doctor along with a nurse carrying some contraption, walked into my room.

"Hello, Jeremy. Well, it looks like you've gotten what you wished for. Neither I nor any of the other doctors see any reason why you don't qualify for the LifeVest. She will instruct you on how it works and tell you everything you need to know," the doctor said.

As the nurse was explaining to me and my parents how to work the defibrillator, I could tell it was going to take a lot of getting used to. Hell, the only time I could take it off was when I showered and even then I had to be monitored by someone to make sure nothing would happen to me. Then the nurse said something that scared the shit out of me, even though she was just doing her job.

"Now Jeremy, this is very important. If the device detects a life-threatening heart rhythm, it will start to beep and then deliver a shock to restore your heart back to normal rhythm. If this ever happens, you should go to the hospital immediately. Understood?" she said.

I kind of sat there for a moment in silence and then said, "Ummm yes. One question. How bad does it hurt when it shocks you?"

"Well, people have told me it's the equivalent of a horse kicking you in the chest, but just hope that doesn't happen," she said.

"Great. One more thing to worry about. Now I'm going to have nightmares about a beeping noise and a horse kicking me in the chest. Just what I want," I thought. Once the nurse was done explaining everything, she then had to teach me how to do CPR. After that, I just had to wait on all my release forms to get filled out and I was home free. Unfortunately, this is the part that always takes forever which meant one thing. More waiting.

Hours later, my nurse finally came in with the papers and my instructions for what I was to do at home. I signed the last one and I was on my way. You know the feeling of getting out for the summer on your last day of school? This was just about that feeling except I had a LifeVest on, a bag holding the battery for the LifeVest, a PICC line in my arm, and a fanny pack holding my portable IV. Nevertheless, it was a great sense of freedom and I couldn't wait to get back home and sleep in my real bed and see all my friends and family I had missed so much.

The drive home was pretty quiet except for our unexpected stop for ice cream. My parents knew how sick I was of hospital food and although I had to eat healthy, a little brownie blast wouldn't hurt anyone. Once we got closer to home, my parents said they had something to show me and instead of taking the route to our house, we detoured and took a route through town. I had no clue what they were doing but once we got to the outskirts of town I could already tell. I saw from a distance that a local business had put on their huge sign a big heart that said "Heart Fore Jeremy" which would become my slogan as I waited for a heart. As we continued through town and down Main Street there were signs in almost every window that said "Heart Fore Jeremy." Some had been printed off and others had been hand drawn by kids throughout the Chanute area. I was in tears. I had no idea how many people cared about me this much. I couldn't go 10 yards without there being a heart with my name on it. It was truly a sight to see and that was only the beginning.

When we got home, I found out that there had been bracelets made that said "Heart Fore Jeremy" and were being sold for my cause. Everyone's pictures on Facebook were being changed to a heart with my slogan on it. People of all ages were mailing me cards telling me good luck and to get well and that everything would be alright. As the week went on, people started to send me "heart healthy" dishes they cooked for me. The small-town support I received is a big reason that I was able to get through everything. The amount of love that my hometown showed for me is something that I'll never forget.

Being at home had its ups and downs. I got to see a few of my friends but most of them were at college so I could only see them on an occasional weekend. The doctors didn't want me doing a lot or to be around a lot of people for fear of me getting sick, so most of the time I spent at home. A nurse came to my house every day to check and see how I was doing and to change my IV and bandages. This got pretty old but she was really nice and I did like someone making sure I was okay. When I showered, I had to make sure my PICC line was all wrapped up because any water on it could lead to potential infection. I was able to take the LifeVest off when I took a shower, but I had to put it right back on when I dried off.

I got really good at video games as the new Call of Duty had just come out. That was cool because I could get on Xbox live and play against my friends at college and was able to talk to them through the headset. Sometimes my dad would come in and attempt to play COD, but after a few sessions he gave up pretty quickly.

A lot of times my family would come out and see me along with my girlfriend, which helped ease the boredom. We would play card games or board games or sometimes just watch a movie. They would do anything to support me and make me feel like everything was going to be alright. If I got too bored at home, my parents would take me for a drive around town or to get a snack. Every so often, we would go to the golf course and have putting and chipping competitions against each other if I felt up to it.

If I wasn't doing any of the above, it probably meant I was praying in the garden. Ever since that night in the hospital, my faith and trust in the Lord had grown immensely. I had started talking to my local priest and got to know him pretty well. To this day we are still really good friends and hang out quite often. He introduced me to some new prayers and gave me some advice on how I could get closer to the Lord and to always trust in Him no matter what. I would sit outside for hours either talking to God or saying the rosary or one of the prayers Father had taught me. I knew my end could be near and I felt that I needed to be closer to the Lord so that I could be in peace when the time came. Come to find out, prayer and trust in the Lord would be the only things that kept me alive in the trying times to come.

Artist Alley was coming up which meant that I had been home for around two or three weeks. This was a big event downtown and I planned on going to it for a bit to see all of my supporters. As far as health goes, I had been feeling as good as the circumstances would permit and the doctors said it would be fine if I went downtown for a few hours. The night before, however, I noticed that I was a lot more tired than usual. I didn't think much of it and just went to bed a little early. The next morning, my life would take a turn for the worst.

As soon as I awoke, I could tell I wasn't feeling as well as the night before. Moments later I started to shake uncontrollably. I went outside and tried to see if that would help but my shaking continued. It was a 90-degree day and no matter how many blankets I put on, I couldn't stop shaking. I knew something was terribly wrong so I yelled for my dad who was outside working. He quickly rushed to the front porch where I was sitting.

"Hey pal, are you okay?" Dad said.

"N-n-n-oooo," I replied.

"Alright, let me call Mom," Dad said.

Mom was downtown at Artist Alley running her shop. When she heard the news she quickly rushed home.

"Jeremy, honey I called the doctors and they said we need to take your vitals and then call them back and let them know the results," Mom said.

"Ok-k-k-aayy," I said weakly.

Mom stuck the thermometer in my mouth and she attempted to put the blood pressure cuff around my arm, but it was no use. I was shaking so badly we couldn't even get it to work.

"Oh my gosh, Son! 103.8! You're burning up! And your lips are blue! We need to get you to the emergency room now," Mom said.

Dad grabbed my arm and helped me to the car as Mom began to call the doctors again and tell them the news. When we arrived at our local ER, I was wheeled in and testing began immediately. The good thing about being in a small town is that you get to know everyone pretty well. It just so happened that the doctor on staff that day was one of the guys I worked out with at the Fitness Center so he knew me quite well.

"I want everything STAT!!" he shouted. "I work out with this kid!"

A few minutes later, some of my family started to arrive. They knew something serious was going on because my parents left work without question on one of the biggest days of the year. After the medicine started to kick in and I began to calm down, a few people at a time were allowed to come in and see me. Father had heard what was going on and came to see me as well. For those of you who don't know Father Bernie, he's a big ole merry fella who has a real deep voice and a way of touching your heart every time you talk to him. He thought it was appropriate to give me the Sacrament of Confession and the Anointing of the Sick as I was in critical condition. I had always known of the Sacrament of the Anointing of the Sick and the seriousness of it, but I never would have guessed I would receive it this young.

A few hours earlier, I had been shaking uncontrollably and although I still felt sick, there was something different. As Father began to rub the oils on me and recite the prayers, I could feel a certain calmness beginning to flow through my body. It felt to me as another way of God saying everything is going to be alright. If there's one thing I've learned from this experience it's that God comes to you when you least expect it. Just when you think all is lost and there is no hope, He will show up in the most mysterious ways.

One of the moments I will always remember from my experience is when my Grandpa Bob walked into my room shortly after Father had left. In his hands he held a rosary and when he saw me laying in pain, tears started to run down his face. He sat down beside me and grabbed my hand and immediately began praying the rosary. I knew my grandpa was a holy man but I never knew of his undying love for our Mother Mary. I could feel God working through him as he recited decade after decade. Once again I was reminded that everything was going to be okay.

When he and my grandma left, he continued to say the rosary in the lobby. Shortly after that the doctor came in.

"Jeremy, we've talked to your doctors at St. Luke's and they want you life-flighted immediately. Unfortunately the weather up by Kansas City is too bad to fly into so we're going to have to ambulance you there. They're going to take good care of you. I'll tell everyone to come say their goodbyes," the doctor said.

Saying goodbye to the people that mean the most to you is one of the hardest things I think I've ever done, especially when you don't know what's to come. I had to do it once in Wichita and now just when I thought things were calming down, I was fighting for my life once again. As I was being wheeled out past the people to the ambulance, tears began to run down my face. I didn't feel well at all but I knew I had to be strong and show my family that I was going to be okay.

Dad was allowed to ride with me in the ambulance and Mom had to drive separately, so she and my cousin Chase followed. The ambulance crew introduced themselves and as they got me situated, I began to get a little excited. "This could be fun," I thought, "I wonder how fast it'll take us to get to Kansas City?" As Dad and I made our wagers, the sirens came on and we were off. I could faintly see the crowd of people waving through the window and I gave a little wave back.

It's funny because even though I went through so much, I could always seem to find a way to laugh and make the most out of a hopeless situation. To this day people ask me how I seemed to stay so strong throughout the whole ordeal and this is a big reason why. Humor and a close relationship with God. If I had focused on all the pain and suffering I went through, I wouldn't be here to write this book today.

A little way through the ride, one of the nurses asked if I would like a Pepsi and some crackers and of course I was all over that. I had been on a heart-healthy diet so this sounded pretty good to me.

All of a sudden my dad turned around and said, "Look Son, a double rainbow!"

"Wow," I said. I had never seen one of those before. It was full of color and stood out beautifully against the storm clouds. The more I thought about it, the more I began to realize it was another sign from God. What did he give Noah after the flood as a promise to never flood the Earth again? A rainbow. And what was he giving me as a promise that everything was going to be okay? A beautiful double rainbow. "God is so good," I thought.

When we arrived at St. Luke's I was expecting to go straight to the fourth floor and be seen by my regular doctors. Instead things went terribly wrong. Apparently they didn't know that I was a heart transplant patient and I had to be taken to the fourth floor because they took me straight to the ER. All I can remember is that it was a complete mess. I was used to things being so organized and this was just complete and utter chaos. I didn't know any of the doctors or nurses on staff. It took them forever to get me into a bed and once they finally did, it took even longer from there because they ran the same damn tests that Chanute did. About four hours later, we finally arrived on the fourth floor.

They situated me in a room and started taking my vitals. Once the basics were done, a doctor arrived and explained what was going to happen in the coming days. Since I was clearly sick, I was to be taken off the list to a Status 7, which as mentioned earlier means that I'm not on the list but I still accrue time. It was now the doctor's job to figure out just what was causing this illness.

I was in the hospital for about a week. It felt like a year. All I could do was keep praying that they would find the problem and take care of it as soon as possible. They ran all sorts of tests on me including an echo, x-rays, and tons of blood work. They finally decided to culture the end of the PICC-line that was in my arm. They ran several cultures for various periods of time until they determined that I had a PICC line infection. Once they knew this, they immediately put me on antibiotics to kill the bacteria.

I was in the hospital for a few more days. Then I was put back on the list and given the okay to go back home and wait. Another PICC line had to be put in, this time in the other arm. They had to monitor me and make sure the antibiotics were working before they could let me go home. Each second was precious because we never knew when I could get the call.

As I filled out the release papers, I wondered how many times I was going to have to go through this. What if I don't get the call for a couple weeks and I have another infection and I have to come back here again? Or what if I my heart can't take it anymore and I die? It's amazing how many things run through a transplant patient's mind on a daily basis. Life can seem impossible at times, but you have to remember that it's a fight. You can either win the fight or you can give up. It's that simple.

The drive home was quiet. We were all pretty exhausted. I took a nap in the backseat and went straight to bed when we got home. The next morning, I did my daily vitals and took my antibiotics. A few members of my family came out to see me. I still wasn't feeling very well so after they left, I took a long nap.

As the days passed, I eventually figured out it would be a lot easier if I tried not to think about getting the call. I didn't have much to do but I kept myself busy. I had been on the list 28 days now and it had been about 10 days since I was released from St. Luke's for my PICC line infection. It was a Sunday afternoon in October, the tenth to be exact, and my Uncle David called and told us he was having a fish fry if we wanted to come out. It was a nice day and my parents thought this would be good for me, if I was up for it.

David had just bought a new house with a lake that wrapped around. It was a great place to go fishing and have a good time. I still had the PICC line in and the LifeVest, which would make things a little difficult, but I wouldn't let that stop me. Once we got there, I immediately grabbed my pole from the back of the truck and headed toward the water. Right off the bat, a fish bit on my spinner bait.

"Fish on!!" I shouted.

"You lucky dog, wait for us!" Dad shouted.

That was one of the best days I had had since I found out I needed a heart transplant. We fished all day long and when we were done, we fried up the fish and ate like kings.

Unfortunately, there was bad cell phone service by David's. As it got close to dark, we decided we better head home. After we got home, my parents and I talked for awhile and then I decided I was going to hit the hay. I was pretty tired from the day's activities. I crawled into bed and before I laid down, I called my girlfriend to tell her how my day went. She lived 3 hours away and was in college, so I called her whenever I could to let her know how things were going. We had been talking for quite a while when all of a sudden an unknown number appeared on my phone.

"Hey babe, hold on a second. Someone is on the other line," I said.

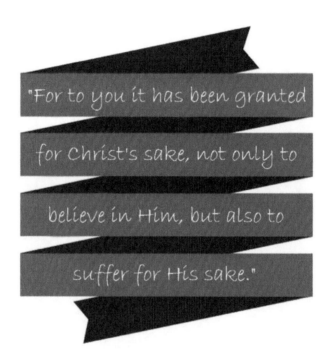

"For to you it has been granted for Christ's sake, not only to believe in Him, but also to suffer for His sake."

Philippians 1:29

Chapter Five

The Call

"**H**ello?" I said in a questioning voice.

"Jeremy, this is Monica from St. Luke's. How are you?" she asked.

"I'm alright. What's up?" I replied.

"We have a heart for you!" she said.

"Really?" I said.

"Yes! I need you to pack your things and come to St. Luke's as soon as possible. Your parents can drive you up. When you get to the hospital, go straight to x-ray and they will inform you on what to do after that. Oh yeah, and don't drink or eat anything starting now," she said.

"Okay. Thank you so much!" I said.

As soon as we were done talking, I switched back to my girlfriend and frantically told her the news.

"Guess what? Guess what?" I said.

"What?" she asked.

"That was St. Luke's! I got a heart!" I said to her in a trembling voice.

She let out a little scream and then said, "Jeremy, that's awesome! Oh my gosh, I'm so excited!"

"I know! Me too! I can't believe it!" I said.

When we finished talking, I hurriedly opened my bedroom door and ran into the living room where my parents were.

"Mom, Dad, I got a heart! I got a heart!" I shouted.

"What?!" they said in disbelief.

"Yeah, they called me when I was on the phone. They said we need to pack our things and drive up there as soon as possible," I said.

I don't think I've ever been more nervous and excited at the same time. Just when I thought I was never going to get the call, it happened. I scrambled into my bedroom and began to pack whatever I thought I would need. A few minutes later, I met my parents at the car and we were off. We were in so much shock we didn't even know what to say.

"I better start calling everyone and tell them the news, don't ya think?" I said to my parents.

"Yeah, that's probably a good idea. I'll start calling, too," said Mom.

We were on the phone the whole way. It was two hours from Chanute to Kansas City and it was storming like crazy. I was just praying we would make it up there in one piece. There were so many emotions and feelings going through my head, it was unreal.

As we were about to arrive at the hospital, reality started to hit me. "This is it," I thought, "I could really die tonight. Or this could be the beginning of a new life. Please, God," I prayed, "Please be with me. I trust in You. Let Your will be done."

When we got to the hospital, we went straight to x-ray and right away we were greeted by a nurse.

"Are you Jeremy?" she said.

"That's me!" I said.

"If you will follow me, I'll take you to get your x-rays and then tell you where you're going to go next," she said.

"Okie doke," I said.

"You must be nervous. I can't imagine what you're feeling right now. It's cool though, you got your call on 10/10/10," she said.

"I know, it's pretty unreal," I said, "I'm just ready for it all to be over."

"I bet, I bet. Well, here we are. I'll see you when you're done," she said.

X-ray only took a few minutes and then I met back with the nurse as we proceeded toward the C-level pre-op room where I would get prepped for surgery. After I completed all the paperwork, I put on a hospital gown and went through a special soap scrub. Cleanliness was a very important part of the surgery. If I were to get an infection because I wasn't sterile, it could cost me my life. Once that was over, I was shown to my bed where I would have my blood drawn. As that was being done, a cardiac surgery resident, some ICU nurses, and my anesthesiologist told me about their part of the surgery. When they finished talking to me, I had to sign my consent that gave St. Luke's permission to perform the heart transplant surgery and for me to receive blood if needed. As I signed that piece of paper, I quietly said, "Well, there's no turning back now."

About ten minutes later my anesthesiologist started two IVs in me, one in each arm. These lines would give me various fluids and medications that I would need throughout the surgery. After giving me some medicine to relax, a catheter was placed into the artery of my wrist, which allowed for continuous monitoring of my blood pressure while I was in the ICU.

It was already past midnight and being on relaxing medicine, I was getting pretty tired. Moments later, a guy who looked like he just got out of bed came up and introduced himself.

"Hello, I'm Dr. Allen. I'll be performing your heart transplant today. I don't want you to worry; we got a good young heart for you. We're just gonna take that old heart out and plug in this new one and you'll be back to normal in no time. Sound good?" he said.

"Sounds perfect," I said in a hazy reply.

"Really?" I thought, "You just got out of bed and you're going to do my heart transplant? Can I get you some coffee or something?" I can't imagine having to do that job. I know they probably get a lot of satisfaction out of it, but there is a lot of pressure riding on you. How would you like to get out of bed at midnight and come do a heart transplant real quick? Doesn't sound like a whole lot of fun to me. And on top of that, he made it sound like no big deal. "Just gonna take that old heart out and slap in a new one, my ass," I thought.

Something else that caught my attention was a guy carrying a cooler. At some point during pre-op, I saw a man carrying a cooler going past my door and a few hours later I saw him carrying it back. I didn't think anything at the time, but I would later find out that my new heart was in that cooler. When they harvest the new heart from the donor, they put it on ice. This allows it to stay healthy for a few hours which gives the harvester time to get it to the hospital where the transplant will take place.

After the surgeon left, I was given a little time with my parents. I had been so busy with prep I hadn't had a chance to talk to them.

"Are you ready, bubba?" Mom said.

"Ready as I'll ever be," I said.

"Don't you worry, pal. You're gonna get that new heart in and you're gonna wake up and feel better than ever," Dad said. "No more being short of breath. Your mom and I have been praying for the perfect heart. I know God won't let us down."

"Thanks you guys. I've been praying a lot lately too and I just want to let you know that whatever happens, I'm ready... All I want is what God wants. Father told me to pray that His will may be done and it's brought me a lot closer to Him. I just want to let you know this. Tell everyone I love them. Whatever happens, I'll be okay. I love you guys," I said in a trembling voice as tears began to roll down my face.

"We love you more than anything, Son," my parents said with teary eyes as they leaned in and hugged me. The amount of love that flowed among us at that moment is truly indescribable. My parents have always been there for me in whatever I chose to do and I could never ask for better ones. I cherished every second of it, as I knew this could be the last time I ever saw them. This was one of those moments that I'll remember for the rest of my life. A few seconds later, a group of nurses arrived.

"Jeremy, it's time," one said.

I turned toward my parents one last time and told them I loved them. As I lay back down on my bed, they began to wheel me into the operating room and I watched my parents fade away in the distance. It was at that moment I knew my life was now in God's hands. As they prepared me for surgery, I said my last words to Him and thought back to the Passion of our Lord.

"Father," I prayed, "Give me strength to continue Your journey and forgive me for all the times I have done You wrong. Please grant me Your mercy and Your grace. I trust in You with all my heart. Whatever Your will is, let it be done. Into Your hands Lord, I commend my spirit."

At that moment, I closed my eyes and left the rest up to God.

"I can do

all things

through Him who

strengthens me."

Philippians 4:13

Chapter Six

Waking Up

I awoke in ICU and everything was a complete blur. I had no clue where I was or why I was even there. To tell you the truth, I can hardly remember the first day after surgery. I was on so many anesthetics and in so much pain that everything was a complete haze.

Looking back on it, I don't know how I ever got through it. I figured I was going to wake up and feel good as new but this, this was the last thing I expected. When I finally came to consciousness the next day, things began to make a little more sense.

I could feel something in my throat and realized it was the breathing tube they talked about before surgery. I could see tons of wires attached to me and stitches running down my chest. When I looked around, I noticed I was in an enclosed room with tons of computers and machines. "Oh my gosh," I thought, "I made it." About that time, I heard a voice. It was my nurse.

"Jeremy, you are in ICU. You just had a heart transplant. Everything went very well. Are you feeling okay?" she asked.

Since the breathing tube was down my throat all I could manage was a nod of my head.

"We're going to try and sit you up in a chair. Once you get sat down, you'll feel a lot better," she said.

I was breathing on my own now so she removed the tube from my throat and began to sit me up and get me moved to a chair. As I sat up I could feel the new heart beating strongly in my chest. When I moved to the edge of the bed and stood up, I noticed how weak I'd become and realized how hard my life would now be. Moving me to the chair was a very difficult process because of all the cords attached to me. By the time I got to the chair, I was completely exhausted and immediately sat down and fell back asleep.

When I awoke a few hours later, I noticed a whole bunch of people looking through the window of my room. No one was allowed in until I was moved to HI-4 due to my critical state, but they could still see me through the glass. As I looked closer, I could see my parents and the rest of my family as well as my coach and the golf team. They all had tears in their eyes and were waving at me. Some of my teammates were making gestures, trying to make me laugh. I was still on a lot of anesthetics and in a lot of pain but I managed to lift my hand up from the chair and give them thumbs up before falling asleep again. It was typical for a transplant patient to fade in and out during the first few days after transplant due to all the medicine.

When I awoke once again, I saw my parents seated beside my bed with masks on. The doctors had allowed them and only them to come inside and see me since they were my guardians. This was a big moment because we weren't sure if we would ever see each other again and here I was alive in the flesh. My throat was feeling better from the breathing tube being removed so I was finally able to talk, although it wasn't much.

"Hey," I said in a raspy voice.

"How are you feeling?" Mom asked.

"I'm alright. Kind of tired and in a lot of pain. How did things go?" I said.

"The doctor's said you did amazing except for a little bleeding. They kept coming out every so often and told us how you were doing. Just try and relax and get some more rest. We love you so much," Mom said.

With a smile on my face I replied, "I love you, too."

A few hours passed and my nurse came back in to check on me. After making sure my vitals were on track, she introduced me to a device called an incentive spirometer. This is a device in which you blow into a tube and try to get the little ball as high as you can. Its job was to get my lungs and breathing back to normal as they had to completely collapse my lungs during surgery and I hadn't been breathing on my own. I was also told that if I felt the urge to cough or sneeze, I was to clutch my heart pillow against my chest to help ease the pain and keep the stitches from coming out.

It had been more than a day now and the discomfort was really starting to hit me. For one, it's very hard to sleep in the ICU as your vital signs are taken frequently and there are so many cords attached to you. I think the anesthetics were wearing off because I began to experience pain throughout my body, especially where they cut me open. When I couldn't take it anymore, I told my nurse and she gave me more pain medicine which helped a lot. As the hours passed, I noticed that my confusion decreased and I seemed to be getting used to things and doing a lot better. My parents were still beside me, comforting me. They kept encouraging me and tried to keep my spirits as high as they could be.

I was nearing my second day in ICU when some nurses and doctors came in for my assessment. I had gotten up a few more times and sat in my chair and walked a few steps, so I was doing very well. It helped that I was in such good shape coming into surgery. After looking over my progress and giving me a quick evaluation, I was released to go to what they called HI-4. This was the after-intensive care room which would be my home for the next few days. It was specially designed for heart transplant patients and had an adjoining room connected to it. If anyone wanted to come into my room, they had to first go in through the adjoining room and sterilize themselves and put on masks and gloves. My immune system was so weak that any form of bacteria could cause me to get very sick and potentially die.

For the first couple days, I was told I could only have immediate family for visitors. If they had any sickness, they weren't allowed to see me. This was very tough because there were so many people that I missed so much and wanted to see. During the first few days in my new room, I had to go through various testing including blood work, chest x-rays, and EKGs. Each morning my weight was checked to make sure I wasn't retaining any fluids. I was also reminded to continue using my incentive spirometer to keep my lungs in tip-top shape.

One thing I remember very well is walking around the hospital with my new heart. I had to put on a mask, which I hated, but whether I felt like it or not, I was encouraged to get up and push myself if I wanted to get out of there sooner. There were a lot of times I didn't have it in me, but my parents would give me the motivation and I would fight through it. I began to think back to Kayla. I remember when she was walking around with her new heart and now here I was with mine. It just didn't even seem possible.

When I returned to my room, I sat down on my bed and started to study my med sheet. If I wanted to get out of here soon, I had to memorize each and every one of the meds I was on. I had to memorize what they were for and when I was supposed to take them. This wouldn't be bad, but starting out I was on 30 different pills. Rejection pills, stomach pills, cholesterol pills, blood pressure pills, you name it. You see, when there is a foreign object inserted into you, your body will reject it. The rejection pills help prevent my body from rejecting my new heart. These pills have horrible side effects, which explains the other 20 some pills I have to take. One pill will cause this so you have to take a pill for that and then that pill causes something. It's a never ending process that isn't a lot of fun. I'm sure some of you have a slight idea of what I'm talking about. And there's no messing up either, because one mistake could cost me my life. It was vital that I learn all my meds.

I can remember the doctors saying, "Now listen, Jeremy. If you don't take your meds correctly or if you mix them up, there's a good chance you will die."

Luckily, by the grace of God my mom had gotten her CNA and CMA licenses right before we found out I needed a new heart, so she was already familiar with a lot of my medicine. As soon as I thought I was ready, she would go down the list and quiz me.

"What are your three rejection pills called?" she would ask.

"Umm Prograf, Prednisone, and Cellcept," I would say.

"Very good," she would reply, "And what does Pravastatin do?"

We did this at least three times a day. At night, one of my nurses would stop by before bed and quiz me as well. To me it just seemed like another test I was studying for except I had to get a perfect score or I flunked. In the end, though, I passed with flying colors.

After I was done with my quiz for the night, I had to say goodbye to my dad. The next day would mark the sixth day since my surgery and they had scheduled a benefit golf tournament, the Jeremy Gant Heart Classic, for me in my hometown. He was going back for that and my mom would stay in the hospital with me. We thought it would be good for one of us to be back in Chanute at the tournament giving my supporters some comfort.

I was pretty excited for the next day even though I couldn't be at the tournament. One of my buddies was going to set up Skype on his laptop in the pro shop and then I would have my laptop in the hospital. This way everyone that hadn't been up to see me could come by the pro shop and say hey. I knew it was going to be a long day, so my mom and I attempted to go to bed right after Dad left. The reason I say attempted is that sleeping after having a new heart put in you is a bit weird. This was one of the first nights that I was actually completely aware of my current state. I began to freak out a bit. You're required to sleep elevated after a transplant for quite a while, which took some getting used to. Besides that, I wasn't used to such a good strong heart in me so hearing it beat kind of freaked me out. It was so strong and so loud that it just didn't seem normal. The nurses assured me everything was fine.

When I awoke the next morning, I went through my daily routine before I got my laptop and turned on Skype. "Blood draw" was first and they filled many tubes with blood and tested for all different kinds of levels. "Vitals" were next which included blood pressure, pulse, respiration, and tem- perature. Not only did I have to take vitals in the morning, I had to take them four other times a day as well. Lastly, I had to get weighed and go through my glorious sponge bath. When all that was done, I ate what I could of my breakfast and then waited on the doctors to come in and see me. After another good report, I finally got situated and turned on my computer. I had heard that people from all over were coming to play in my tournament so I was excited to see them all. Once Mom and I got the okay, we fired up Skype. Sure enough, there was the pro shop full of people waiting to see me.

It was so nice to finally see everyone together with smiles on their faces. I had gotten so used to the sight of people crying that I forgot what it was like. I'll admit, the world we live in today is so full of hatred, but to see so many people come together made my experience well worth it.

For the rest of the day I stayed on Skype and talked to everyone I could, even if it was just for a few minutes. Not only that but I had tons of visitors in the hospital as well. By the time the tournament was over I was completely exhausted and had to take a nap before the auction started. Some of my friends got a lot of cool raffle items together to help raise money. These included autographs from famous people and a round of golf with Tom Watson and me, to name a few. Everyone was so generous at the auction and really made it a lot of fun to watch. When it was all said and done, they raised more than $28,000 for my foundation. I was in shock. It is truly amazing what people can do when they have love in their hearts.

It was now October 17th and I was nearing the end of my stay at the hospital. Despite a good night's rest, I was still extremely exhausted from the day before. I would learn very quickly that fatigue would become a constant battle for me in the years to come if I didn't stay on top of things. Nevertheless, today would turn out to be a really fun day as my grandparents and my cousin were coming to see me. They had been at the hospital as often as they could, but this would be the first time they actually got to sit down and talk to me since the transplant.

When they arrived, I could tell they were extremely happy to see me up and moving. They had brought tons of games for us to play which were a lot of fun. If we weren't playing games, someone was walking around the floor with me, helping me rebuild my strength. It was so nice to finally have a feeling that everything just might be okay. I had a long way to go, but so far things were looking up.

When it was time for them to go, I said my goodbyes and told them I'd be seeing them in a couple days. It doesn't seem like a long time but I had my first biopsy in the morning and judging by the way Kayla talked about it, I was in for a real treat. For those of you who don't know what a biopsy is let me explain it to you.

A biopsy after a heart transplant is a little different than other biopsies. This biopsy is done to test whether or not your heart is being rejected. First, the cardiologist injects the area on the right side of your neck with an anesthetic that burns like crazy. Next, he inserts a tube into the carotid artery and threads a biopsy forcep through the tube into the right side of the heart. He then snips four or five pieces of the heart and drops them in a tube for testing. When this happens, you can feel your heart fluttering and skipping beats, which is normal but completely insane. After all the samples are obtained, he withdraws the tube and places a bandage over the site. During the first six months after transplant, biopsies are done quite often. After that they begin to slow down.

When I awoke the next day, I went through my morning routine except this time I couldn't have breakfast until after the biopsy. I hadn't slept much the night before because I couldn't stop thinking about the biopsy. Not only that, my biopsy was scheduled at 7 a.m. so it was really early for me.

After listening to the nurse's instructions, I said goodbye to my parents and they assured me everything was going to be just fine. A few minutes later, a guy in scrubs came to my door pushing a wheelchair.

"Jeremy Gant," he shouted.

"That's me," I said.

I was fairly silent on the ride down to the operating room, partially because I was still asleep, but also because I was a little nervous. When we arrived I was instructed to take my shirt off and lay on the table. All I can remember was it was freezing in there. They finally got me some warm blankets and then strapped me down to the table and prepped me for surgery. A few minutes later, the doctor performing the biopsy came in and introduced himself.

"Hello, I'm Dr. Magalski. I'll be doing your biopsy today," he said. "It's going to be real quick and easy. You have nothing to worry about."

If I had a nickel for every time I heard that.

He put a blue sheet on me with a slit over the insertion point, so nothing would get infected.

"Alright Jeremy, you're going to feel a stick and a burn. Are you ready?" the doctor said.

"Yup," I said nervously.

Sure enough, the needle part wasn't bad but the burn took some getting used to.

"You doing okay?" the doctor asked.

"Yes sir," I said.

It really wasn't that bad, but the worst was yet to come.

"Okay, now I'm going to insert the tube. You feel anything?" the doctor said.

"Nothing," I said.

"Good. Now we're going to draw some blood and then we'll begin getting the pieces of your heart," he said. "So I heard you were a golfer?"

"Yeah that's me," I said. "I play at Newman University in Wichita."

"That's really cool. I try to golf but it doesn't work out too well," he said with a laugh. "Alright we're ready to get those pieces. You're going to feel a few extra beats when we snip the pieces but it's totally normal, okay?"

"If you say so," I said.

When that wire touched my heart and I started feeling those extra beats I almost jumped off the table. It was one of the weirdest feelings I have ever experienced. It's something you just have to feel for yourself to understand.

As soon as he snipped the fourth and final piece of my heart, I breathed a huge sigh of relief.

"Okay Jeremy, we're all done," he said. "I just have to pull the sheath out and put a bandage on your neck and you're good to go. You did great!"

"Thank you so much, doctor," I said.

Once the bleeding stopped and the bandage was on my neck, I sat down in my wheelchair and was pushed back up to my room. "Thank God that's over," I thought.

When I got back, I could tell my parents were anxiously awaiting my return. As soon as they saw me, they ran up and gave me a big hug.

"How'd it go, honey?" Mom asked.

"It wasn't as bad as I thought. The doctor did a good job. It seemed like it went pretty fast," I told them.

"Good. We were so worried. Your breakfast should be here shortly. Why don't you lie down and get some rest until it gets here," Mom said.

As soon as I finished eating my breakfast, I was out. My job the rest of the day was to rest, walk around, and use my spirometer. I only had a couple of visitors later in the day, but other than that it was pretty boring. I was just ready to get out of the hospital and on with my life.

The next day, I was awake bright and early. If I wanted to get out of there by noon, I had a lot of things that needed to be done. Papers had to be signed, instructions had to be given, and farewells had to be said. After breakfast, I was visited by many doctors and nurses. The first few talked a lot about infections and how to avoid getting sick. Because of all the medicine I'm on, my immune system is suppressed which puts me at high risk for getting an infection. They said it's very important that I wash my hands frequently and avoid people who are sick. Also they said it was a good idea to stay away from public places for quite a while. If I start to cough or have a fever while at home, I am supposed to immediately call them because even the slightest illness could result in death.

When that set of doctors left, I had some others come in to talk to me about nutrition and exercise. It was very important that I have an exercise program and keep my heart in shape. They weren't particularly worried in my case but they still had to stress the importance. After a month, I was to have cardiac rehab set up in my hometown so I could start that. It was also stressed that I eat and drink right. They had gotten me this new heart and it was my job to keep it healthy.

One of my main doctors came in for the last time to go over any unanswered questions. After that, he bid me farewell. I couldn't drive or swing a golf club for at least six weeks or until my sternum was fully healed. Due to all the medicine and everything that had gone on, I was once again reminded that I could experience severe mood swings and depression. If anything got too out of hand, I was encouraged to see a psychologist.

"It's been a pleasure, Jeremy. I bet you're ready to get home," the doctor said.

"Yes I am. You guys were great and all but I think it's time I go," I said.

"Well your nurse should be in shortly with your release papers and instructions. Once you get those signed, you're free to go. I expect an autograph when you get on the PGA," the doctor said.

"Consider it done, Doc. Have a good one," I said.

"Take care, Jeremy," he said.

After what seemed like an eternity, my nurse finally walked in with my papers. I gave her my John Hancock and I was home free.

And He did not let him, but He said to him,

"Go home to your people and report to them

what great things the Lord has done for

you, and how He has mercy on you."

Mark 5:19

Chapter Seven

Home Sweet Home

It's amazing how life works. One day you're watching cartoons at Grandma's house and the next you're in a hospital bed fighting for your life. And when you think all hope is lost, you're on your way home with a new heart. This is all I could seem to think about. So many things had happened so fast that it just didn't even seem possible. All I could do was keep praying for God's will and hope that the worst was behind me.

As we pulled up at our house, we were greeted by my grandparents and a big sign in our yard that read, "Welcome Back Jeremy!" Despite being extremely tired, I was very glad to see them. They had cleaned and disinfected our entire home so that I had the least chance of getting sick. They had also elevated my bed just like the doctors had said to do. "I don't know what I'd do without them," I thought. "They are so good to me."

I went straight to my room after they left, crawled under the covers, and closed my eyes. It was such a good feeling to finally be back in my own bed. At last I could go to sleep and not have to worry about getting on the list or getting a heart in time or getting stabbed with a needle at 5 a.m. It had been a long journey and I was ready for a break.

The next morning marked the first day of my new life at home. It also marked the beginning of a fight I would continue for the rest of my life. A lot of people think that the story ends there. They think that I finally got new heart and now I can go back to my normal life. Come to think of it, that's what I thought, too. But with each passing day, my mind quickly changed.

That morning, I ventured toward the bathroom to take a shower. I had only been able to take sponge baths in the hospital but now the doctors had approved me for a real shower. I was looking forward to this immensely. I normally had tubes attached to me and paper bags wrapped around them. Now there was nothing but a scar down my chest.

I stepped into the shower and everything was going fine. Better than fine. The hot water pouring down on me felt amazing and having privacy was even better. "Wow, I've needed this," I thought. All of a sudden I began to feel extremely weak and got light-headed. I completely lost my vision and collapsed on the shower floor. I yelled out for my parents and they came rushing in immediately. As they picked me up and dried me off, they shouted, "Are you okay, Son? What happened?"

"I'm, I'm fine. I got tired and fell," I mumbled softly.

Apparently the combination of my weakened state and the hot water pouring down had caused me to pass out. Something as simple as a shower was now another obstacle to overcome. Until I got my strength back, I would have to shower sitting down.

When I had recovered from my fall, I noticed I was extremely tired and had very little energy. I'm sure my body was still catching up on sleep and healing itself but I didn't think I would feel this bad. I was supposed to have my life back now. I was supposed to wake up from transplant and feel full of energy and better than I had ever felt before... I felt like shit. Nevertheless I knew I had to push myself and keep moving forward. Giving up wasn't in my vocabulary.

Later that day, my parents went with me on my walk. It was so nice walking outside instead of around a hospital all day. I was still pretty tired from the morning's experience, but I wanted to get out of the house. I knew I couldn't make it very far but I had to do the best I could. As I stepped onto the grass, I slowly made my way toward our mailbox, about 50 yards away. I figured this would be a good starting point. Everything was fine at first but about halfway to the mailbox, I felt a familiar feeling. My heart started to pound and my legs grew weak. My vision faded and soon I was walking blind.

"We have to turn around. I don't feel good," I said to my parents.

"Son, we aren't even to the road yet. We have to push this new heart. We won't let anything happen to you," Mom said.

I kept on walking in hopes that I would start to feel better. Each step was a fight, but I kept thinking back to Jesus carrying the cross. "God, please give me strength," I prayed. We made it another 50 yards. My parents could tell I was going to collapse.

"Alright, let's go in. Tomorrow we will see if we can go even farther," my dad said.

After a short rest, we made our way back to the house. They had to practically carry me, but eventually we reached the front door. I sat down on the porch to catch my breath while my parents went inside to get me a glass of water. I took a couple big gulps and breathed a sigh of relief. Then my parents noticed something else.

"Why are you shaking like that?" Mom asked.

"I can't help it. I don't know," I said.

"Well we're going to have to talk to the doctor. Things just don't seem right," Mom said.

It was about this time that depression started to set in. I hadn't even been home a day and already, this new life was kicking my ass. I couldn't shower. I couldn't walk. Hell, I could barely drink a glass of water without spilling it on me. I knew that things were going to be tough, but I didn't imagine anything like this. What if I got a bad heart? How long was this going to last? I really didn't want to go through this again. This wasn't anything like they said it would be. They didn't tell me any of this! I was angry and frustrated already.

Mom got on the phone with the doctor's office and pretty soon she handed the phone to me.

"Jeremy, this is Jodie. How are you?" she asked.

"Not the best," I replied.

"Well, I don't want you to worry. Being weak is normal after transplant. You just went through a huge surgery. It's going to take some time for you to get back to the strength you had before. You're on a lot of pills and they have a lot of nasty side effects. Your shakiness is from one of these nasty pills called Prednisone. This is a bad drug but you will get off of it eventually. After a year, you'll get off some of these pills and everything will start looking up! You stay strong and stay in touch if you need anything okay?" she said.

"Alright, I'll do that. Thank you," I said.

"Why the hell don't they tell you these things before transplant? They made it sound so easy. 'You're going to get this new heart and feel better than ever! Oh yeah, the first year is going to be hell, though.' What if I didn't want to go through all this?" I said furiously to my mom.

"Jeremy, don't talk like that. Things are going to get better, I promise. You have to stay strong, honey. Remember the Passion? I think now would be a good time to go pray and talk to God about your problems," she said.

I thought about that for a moment.

"You're right, Mom. I'm gonna go do that right now."

As I ventured back to my room, I knelt down and thought about God and His plan for me. One of the greatest lessons I've learned is to never let God out of your life and that's exactly what I was doing. I wasn't trusting His plan for me. It's really easy to put Him on the backburner when things are going well and to blame everything on Him when things are going badly. I was on a lot of different medications that caused a lot of these emotions I was feeling, but that was no excuse. God never gives anyone something they can't handle. I had to believe in His plan and keep moving forward.

The next day I awoke to my Dad knocking on my bedroom door.

"Breakfast is ready!" he shouted.

I could smell the undeniable aroma of bacon. Sure enough, Dad had made me bacon and eggs that morning which was my favorite. About that time the alarm on my phone went off reminding me to take my meds. Every day at 9 a.m. and 9 p.m. I had to remember to take my meds no matter what I was doing. After I downed my pills, I went to the kitchen and began to gobble up my food and a glass of orange juice.

When I finished eating, I watched TV for a bit and continued to strengthen my lungs with the spirometer. I was feeling a lot better today.

"Well Son, we probably should go for another walk," Dad said. "We gotta keep pushing your heart like the doctor said to do."

"Alright, let's go far today," I told him. "I'm feeling pretty good."

"I like that attitude," Dad said.

Having barely made it past the mailbox the previous day, my new goal was to more than double that. We stepped off the front porch and began making our way past the mailbox towards the road. Once we got to the road, I just kept on going. Once we made it past my neighbor's house, I went even farther.

"How are you feeling now?" Dad asked me.

"My heart's beating pretty hard and I'm a little out of breath, but I feel alright," I replied.

"Well, you did good. We better not go too much farther or you won't be able to make it back," Dad said.

When we got back to the house, I sat down on the couch to catch my breath. I was a little light-headed, but it was an improvement from the day before. A few hours later, my parents and I ventured out to the golf course. I couldn't swing a club yet, but I could putt and chip. It was so nice to just be able to do some sort of golfing again. Being cooped up in a hospital room for so long will make you want to stay on the golf course forever. I was a little rusty, but at least my short game would get a lot better until I could swing a club again.

After an hour or so, we went by Sonic and then headed home to get ready for bed. It was a little early but I was still catching up on sleep. Plus, tomorrow would be a very busy day.

My uncle Tim and a whole bunch of people had gotten together and decided to have a benefit poker run for me. He had called me a few days before and asked if I could stand down on Main Street and wave as all of the Harley riders drove by to show my gratitude for what they were doing. Of course I said I would. About noon, we all headed down to Main Street and almost immediately we could hear them coming. They all roared past me with smiles on their faces and pipes a-blazing. It was a really cool sight to see. Once again, I was in awe of all the support I was receiving.

Later that day, after things had cooled down from all the excitement, it was time for church. This was a very big deal for me. It would mark the first time I had gone to church since receiving my new heart. I knew it would be a special evening as everyone in the congregation had been praying for me. The only bad thing was that church was a public place with a lot of germs, so I had to wear a mask. For a couple of months, I couldn't go anywhere without wearing a mask. Nevertheless, I was excited, to be in God's house where I belonged.

When my family and I walked through the doors, heads immediately began to turn. As we made our way to our seats, you could see all the people gazing in disbelief with big smiles on their faces. God had answered their prayers.

I had been in touch with Father, so he knew I was going to be there that evening. I had a pretty good idea he was going to have something special planned, but I never imagined the impact it would have on me.

Once Father got to his sermon, he paused for a moment. As tears began to run down his face, he said, "Brothers and Sisters, tonight we are in the presence of something special. This young man we have with us tonight has demonstrated an immense amount of courage and faith in the fight for his life. I would like to welcome Jeremy Gant back to our parish."

Everyone in the church stood up and gave a huge ovation. I was so deeply touched; I grabbed both of my parents' hands and just let it all out. With tears streaming down my face, I stood up and gave a wave to everyone in the church and a nod to Father. When I sat back down and the cheering subsided, Father gave an amazing sermon of my story and how it related to the Gospel that day, which happened to be God's will. I sat there reliving every moment of my journey and watched as the people followed along. "I am truly one lucky kid," I thought.

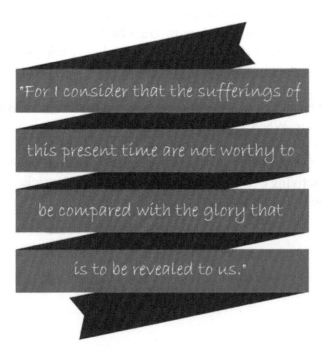

"For I consider that the sufferings of this present time are not worthy to be compared with the glory that is to be revealed to us."

Romans 8:18

Chapter Eight

Up and Down

B EEP, BEEP, BEEP!! "Oh my gosh, this is too early," I thought as I hit the snooze button on my alarm.

"Jeremy, you better wake up. It's already 6:30!" Mom shouted.

"Alright, alright," I groaned.

If you couldn't tell, I'm not a morning person at all. Even if I get 12 hours of sleep, I still feel like crap. I thought having my heart transplant would help, but so far it was having the opposite effect.

When we were all finally ready, we hopped in the cold car and made our way to the hospital. It was time for another biopsy. I was still half asleep, so I was just following my parents' lead. I wondered why they couldn't do biopsies in the afternoon. That would make my life so much easier.

To my surprise, everything went extremely well that day. We didn't have to wait much, my blood work went well, and all the nurses and doctors were really cool. On top of that, my buddy Daniel had his biopsy scheduled the same day. He was a heart transplant patient, too. Whenever we were both free, we would sit down and talk about how our week went and what new challenges we had to face. His mom came too, so she would sit down with my parents and keep them company. It definitely made things go a lot more quickly, that was for sure.

We said our goodbyes and headed to get something to eat. Each time I had a biopsy, I had to fast from midnight on. By the time everything was done, I was extremely hungry. When we got done eating, we ran a few errands then decided we better head home. It had been a good day, but everyone was pretty worn out.

As the weeks went by, I stuck to my daily routine. Eventually, I was able to stand up and shower. After about a week, I could walk almost a mile. All of my biopsies continued to come back perfect and for a little while things seemed like they were finally looking up. Then out of the blue, everything collapsed all at once.

I mentioned earlier that the thirty-some meds I was taking had some side effects, but I didn't go into detail. After about a month, these side effects really started to kick in. My acne was getting out of control. I fought constant fatigue and diarrhea. Hell, I lost 10 pounds in a matter of days because whatever went in went right back out. That became a problem because I had to check the stool and make sure none of my meds were in there. Headaches started to come on as well as mood changes and extreme weakness. I shook all the time and my appetite skyrocketed. And let's not forget the swelling in my body and the constant nausea. For the first year, I went through hell. My good days were days a normal person would feel like going to the hospital and dying. But I wasn't about to let people know this. Whenever someone asked how I was doing, I always replied with, "I'm doing really good!"

You can only imagine what all these things do to a 19 year-olds mind. I can't tell you how many days I was pissed off at the world, yelled at everyone around me, and straight up wished I was dead. I remember my dad and I talking one day, debating whether meeting my Maker would have been better than going through all this.

I was only a month out at this point and already I was drowning in a pool of misery. I had no clue it was going to be this tough. I guess that's what I get for believing people that had never been through what I was going through. Did you know that around 90 percent of transplant patients are on antidepressants or see a psychologist? Yeah, I soon found that out, but I wasn't about to go down that road. In my eyes, seeing a shrink who doesn't know shit about your situation was a sign of weakness and failure. That's not me. Although I was on an antidepressant, I wasn't going to give in completely just yet.

It had been more than a month since my transplant, so cardiac rehab had begun. I wasn't too crazy about the whole deal, but I figured it would get me out of the house. Every morning for three days a week, I went to the hospital and worked out for about an hour. I was required to do 15 minutes on the bike, elliptical and treadmill while my vitals were monitored on a computer. Everyone was really nice and things were going well, but it just wasn't the place for me. I was a bodybuilder not an old person recovering from a bypass surgery. I bet I was the youngest person they had by at least 30 years. It was only a few weeks before I contacted my doctors and they cleared me to work out on my own. I still couldn't lift a lot of weight, but at least I could go to a real gym and get my self-esteem back.

Another couple weeks passed by and again things seemed to look up. As a matter of fact, I was just positive I was done with most of my struggles. A band by the name of Stars Go Dim had heard my story and had come to Chanute to perform a benefit concert for me. One of our local boys, Skye Smeed opened up for them and it turned out to be one hell of a night.

Then one day out of the blue, I got a call from the Oklahoma State golf coach.

"Hello, Jeremy?" Coach asked.

"Yeah, this is him," I answered.

"It's Mike McGraw, the head men's golf coach at Oklahoma State University. How are you doing?" he asked.

"Uhh, I'm doing alright. How are you? It's been a while," I said.

"I've been really well. Randy Pryor from Chanute emailed me and told me that you just had a heart transplant. When he said your name and that you went to my golf camp a few years back, I immediately remembered you. That's pretty crazy," he said.

"Yeah, it was definitely a wakeup call," I said.

"I bet. Listen, I don't know much about your situation but I was wondering what you were doing December 1st?" he said.

"Nothing, as far as I know. Why?" I answered.

"Well, Peter Uihlein, who just won the U.S. Amateur and plays golf here at Oklahoma State, is going to be here along with all the other guys on the team. They were wondering if you wanted to come down to Stillwater and play golf with them," Coach said.

"That would be a dream come true!!" I replied excitedly.

"Good, well I'll keep in touch and let you know more details in the next few days. Plan on coming that morning though. It'll be a fun day," Coach said.

"Are you kidding me?" I thought. "I get to play golf with all the OSU boys? This is crazy!!" You see, growing up I was (and still am) a diehard Oklahoma State fan. I wanted to play golf there my whole life, but I just wasn't quite good enough. At any rate, I still followed the program and when I heard this news, it was like the equivalent of a basketball fan meeting Michael Jordan. I mean come on! These guys are some of the best college golfers in the world. When I told my parents the news, they couldn't believe it either. Despite all the hardships I was going through, I was one lucky kid.

When the OSU day came, I was more nervous than if I was tied going into the last hole of the Masters. I had hit a few balls, but I was still far off my game. I knew it wasn't about competition, but I still wanted to show them what I had. When we arrived in Stillwater, things started to look familiar. We turned into Karsten Creek Country Club and I remembered the long, winding road back to the golf course. Once the trees opened up, I could see the familiar site of the breathtaking clubhouse overlooking the 18th green.

We stepped out of the car from our long three-hour drive and made our way toward the clubhouse doors. As soon as we opened them, I saw Coach McGraw and Peter Uihlein standing next to the U.S. Amateur trophy with big smiles on their faces.

"Jeremy, I'd like you to meet Peter Uihlein," Coach said.

"Hey man, what's going on?" I said in disbelief.

"Not a lot. You ready to go play some golf?" he asked excitedly.

"Yes, I am! Let's do it," I replied.

As Peter and I got our clubs loaded onto a cart, Coach McGraw gave my parents a tour of the clubhouse and the famous trophy hall. When we were warmed up, my parents said their goodbyes and we were off.

That was one of the best days I can remember having after transplant. It was as if everything I had been dealing with just went away. Peter and I talked all day long about all kinds of things. He would ask about my story and then I would ask him if he was getting nervous about playing in the Masters. To top it all off, I played pretty well.

As we were making our way up the 18th hole, I could see my parents by the green watching us come in. Peter and I both hit good shots and we got a tiny ovation. I can only imagine how it felt for my parents to finally see their son back on a golf course. And playing with the best amateur golfer in the country. It must have been as much a blessing for them as it was for me.

When we finished, Peter gave me an autographed picture of him holding the U.S. Amateur trophy, along with a team photo with all their autographs. We said our goodbyes and then Coach took my parents and me out to eat before we left. We ate at a pizza place in Stillwater and I demonstrated my eating skills to Coach. Little did I know, he was the world's fastest eating human alive.

Coach gave me an official team hat and said he would be in touch. I told him thanks for everything and that he had made all my dreams come true. His last words were, "Don't worry, there will be more," which got me wondering.

We got home late that night, but it didn't matter because I slept all the way home. I still couldn't believe what had just happened. Then again, neither could anyone else. I had been through hell, but at least there were some good things happening now.

The next few weeks went by fairly quickly. My biopsies were moved to every other week and my pill situation was starting to get lined out. Apparently it takes awhile to figure out how your body reacts to certain types of pills. It was really good to finally have a sense of the word "normal" in my life.

The holidays went really well, too. I didn't ask for a lot that Christmas, as I was just grateful to be alive, but of course I got plenty of gifts. It was really nice to spend the holidays with my family. We had all grown closer throughout my whole ordeal. It made this Christmas extra special.

In January we entered the year of 2011. Since the doctors wouldn't let me go back to Newman this semester, I planned on taking classes at our local college so that I could stay caught up. They were just afraid that since I still didn't have a very strong immune system and it was flu season, it wouldn't be a very good idea to go back. I was fine with it. I missed my friends, but it was good to be home.

One day after I had gotten my books for the upcoming semester, I noticed that the left side of my body was starting to hurt. I didn't think much of it but a few days later I started to run a high fever. "Great," I thought, "My body decides to get sick right when classes are about to start." I told my Mom and she gave me some Tylenol, but things just kept getting worse. I tried to shake it off, but on the night of the 19th, I awoke to the most pain I had ever experienced in my entire life. It was like someone was stabbing me in the side with a knife.

"Aahhh!! Gahh!!" I shouted as I clutched my side for dear life. My parents came running into my room.

"Jeremy, are you okay?" Mom said.

"No...I need to go to the Emergency Room now! It hurts so bad!" I screamed.

The drive to the hospital was a long one. I was in severe pain the whole way and it just seemed to get worse. We had learned after our many visits to St. Luke's to call ahead and we did just that. I didn't want to go through another emergency room fiasco. When we finally arrived, I could hardly breathe the pain was so bad. It was late, I was tired, and I just wanted the pain to stop.

We got admitted into a small room no bigger than a prison cell. When the nurse came in, I immediately yelled out in pain and she got the IV going. After taking my vitals, she injected some pain medicine into my IV. It was immediate relief. I was told to rest for the night and in the morning, we would begin testing.

The next day was a long one. Several different blood tests were administered and a chest x-ray was done. After lunch, the doctor came in with the results.

"Jeremy, I'm afraid the chest x-ray shows nothing at all. I believe the next step is going to be a CAT scan," he said.

That afternoon, I was taken down to the CAT scan room and went through that whole process. If you aren't familiar with it, it's like something from the future. You lay down on a table and slide into a machine that spins around you really fast and makes you feel like you are being sent to the future. It is kind of cool actually, but at this point I just wanted to get it over with.

After the test was complete, I was wheeled back to my room and given more pain medication. My pain wasn't as bad, but it was starting to come back again. I would have to wait till the next day to find out exactly what was wrong with me. If the CAT scan couldn't find it, I didn't know what was going to happen. On top of that, my Dad had to go back to Chanute to work and my Mom had begun to get sick as well. It would be a very long night.

The next morning the doctor came in bright and early with my results.

"I am afraid the problem was hiding behind your heart. That is why the chest x-ray showed nothing. You have a severe case of pneumonia and will have to stay with us until it subsides. We will get you started on some medication that should take care of it. In the mean time, you get some rest," the doctor said.

"Wow," I thought, "this is going to be a very long stay. Am I ever going to have a normal life again?"

That week went by very slowly. Mom got some medicine to take care of her sickness. It would be just us two for the time being, but Dad would call every day to check up on me. The rest of my family and friends would too. I will say one thing; it is very helpful to have a good support system like I have. I cannot imagine going through all of this by myself.

When we got back home just shy of two weeks later, I was extremely exhausted. I had to get back in the routine of the biopsies and my new life. On top of that, I started school at our local college the next week. Fortunately, it didn't turn out that bad. I got back in my routine and did my very best to not get sick. I exercised every day and ate as healthy as I could. Life was finally starting to get back to normal, or at least as normal as it could get for me.

I now had the chance to write a letter to my donor family. It was something that I had thought a lot about and decided it was time. They couldn't receive the letter until a year had passed due to the grieving process, but at least it would be there ready for them to read.

I sat down with my parents and we discussed what we wanted to say. I couldn't give a lot of detail about myself, but I could give all the necessary information. This was such a bittersweet subject to write about because even though my life was saved, they lost a loved one and were dealing with that heartbreak. It took me several hours to come up with exactly what I wanted to say. A lot of emotions were going through my head. I tried my best to put myself in their shoes and to make the letter as cheerful as possible. After several hours of editing and re-editing, we decided that it was complete and sent it in to the hospital. I would just have to wait for a response and pray that when the time was right, they would write back.

As the days went by, I continued with my routine and everything seemed to be going as planned. But on March 16, 2011, something truly amazing happened. I was in Springfield visiting my girlfriend when I got another call from Coach McGraw. My heart leapt as I picked up the phone.

"Jeremy, this is Coach. How you are?" he said.

"I am doing well, Coach. What's going on?" I said.

"Can you be here in the morning?" he said. "I have something special planned for you."

"Alright Coach. I'll be there," I said excitedly.

I don't know how far it was from Springfield, Missouri to Stillwater, Oklahoma but I know it's a long way. Regardless, after what Coach did for me the first time, I knew this was going to be something out of this world.

I awoke the next morning at 4 a.m. and began my journey to Karsten Creek. It is a good thing someone invented the GPS because there is no way I could have made it there without it. I was so excited, yet so tired at the same time. What could Coach possibly have up his sleeve this time?

After what seemed like an eternity, I arrived at Karsten Creek on a glorious Wednesday morning. As I stepped out of my car and stretched my legs my heart began to beat really fast, but not because something was wrong. I knew something awesome was about to happen.

I opened the double doors to the majestic clubhouse overlooking the 18th green and made my way to Coach's office. When I opened the door my heart nearly stopped. There sitting on Coach's desk with his hat on backwards and his Puma gear glowing was Rickie Fowler.

"Jeremy, how was the drive?" Coach asked with a big smile on his face.

"Ummm, it was alright. Little tired," I said in disbelief.

"Well, I'd like you to meet Rickie Fowler," he said.

This was the start of one of the best days of my life. We sat in Coach's office for quite a while just talking. As the morning progressed, we made our way to the golf course. My game had gotten a little better, but I was still pretty rusty. Nevertheless, my competitive spirit wanted to show Rickie just how much fight this transplant patient had.

There were two moments that day I will never forget. The first one occurred on the second hole. Rickie and I hit our drives right beside each other and left our approaches 20 or so yards short of the green. The pin was tucked on the front and we had no green to work with. What happened next really put into perspective just how good these guys are. I was away and decided to hit a bump and run due to the tight lie I had in the fairway. I knocked it to about seven feet and figured Rickie would take the same approach. Instead, he pulled out his lob wedge, opened the blade, and hit this spinning flop shot that landed five feet behind the hole and spun back to about six inches. It was safe to say I had my work cut out for me.

The second moment happened near the end of the round on the 15th hole. It was a long par 3 playing close to 220 yards with a slight crosswind. Rickie, of course, knocked it to 30 feet like it was nothing. I, on the other hand, was a bit nervous, but tried to shake it off. I pulled out my 4 iron and gave it a mighty whack. It was the best struck golf shot I had hit in a long time.

As it landed on the green and rolled up next to the pin, I picked up my tee and gave Rickie a "Take that!" look. He smiled, gave me some knuckles and told me nice shot. It was one of the most fulfilling moments I have ever experienced.

I got the opportunity to spend the next few days just hanging out with Rickie and the rest of the OSU guys. I was getting the chance to live the life I had dreamed of since I was a kid and that is something I will never forget. Coach McGraw did so many things for me that I will never be able to repay. Rickie and the rest of the OSU players demonstrated just how great a bunch of guys they really are. To take a complete stranger and make him one of your own is really something special. I will never forget what they did for me and will be forever grateful.

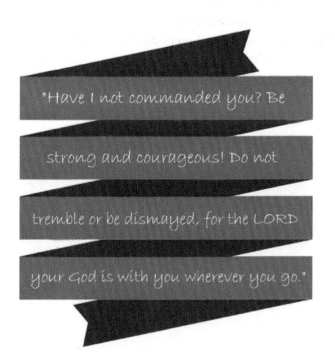

"Have I not commanded you? Be strong and courageous! Do not tremble or be dismayed, for the LORD your God is with you wherever you go."

Joshua 1:9

Chapter Nine

The Fight Continues

As August rolled around I made my way back to Newman to prepare myself for the upcoming year. It was nice to get back into the swing of things; I had missed being at college with all of my friends. The golf season, however, proved to be a very challenging experience. I had come a long way but was still far from where I needed to be. Most tournaments were 36 holes the first day and I was still not physically able to carry my bag for that amount of time. I was approved for a pull cart, but no one really knew how much this would hurt me. I wanted to be just like everyone else, but after the first few tournaments I knew that my life had truly changed. I was physically and mentally exhausted. Between going to school, golf practice and tournaments, I was worn out. My golf game was nowhere near where it needed to be and those negative thoughts kept coming into my mind. Just when I thought my life was beginning to get back to normal…

As my one-year anniversary approached, my life continued on its rollercoaster. On September 28th, 2011, we hosted the 2nd annual Jeremy Gant Heart Classic in Chanute. This year would be a lot different because I would actually be there to see all of the people supporting my cause.

My competitive spirit got the best of me. I decided that I would play in the tournament and hit the first tee shot in front of all my supporters. This was a two-man scramble, which meant I needed a partner. Of course, I knew this ahead of time and had made a few phone calls. Coach McGraw had agreed to play with me in the tournament and experience firsthand what Chanute was all about.

I was ecstatic about this opportunity and had been practicing hard on my golf game. I knew this was something more than just a round of golf. This was an opportunity to connect with those who had shown me so much support.

As I stepped up on the tee, my heart was pounding. I was more nervous than ever. I had the Oklahoma State golf coach as a partner in my own tournament and a crowd of people surrounding us. As the crowd quieted down, I went through my routine and swung away.

Coach and I had a great time and exchanged jokes throughout the round. Everyone was enjoying themselves and I couldn't have been more pleased. We even ended up placing pretty high. But in the midst of all that, something hit me.

I would never actually be able to live my dream of playing golf at Oklahoma State for Coach McGraw. I would most likely never be on the PGA tour playing against Tiger Woods and Phil Mickelson. How could I possibly be feeling this way? So many great things had happened to me in the past year, yet something was still missing.

This would be the start of a part of my life very few people know about. I have always tried my best to be a positive person and make the best of my situation, but it is only fair that you know my whole story.

I have read a lot of inspiring stories from people around the world who have encountered adversity and beat it. I have witnessed firsthand some of the greatest people imaginable. But I feel like they never really tell you the full story. They never talk about the times they failed and almost lost it all. I would be lying to you if I ended my book here, so let's get on with the rest of the story.

Despite the recent events in my life, I was still a kid. I had just survived a major surgery and was now thrown back into college life. People tried to tell me that I was "normal" again and just like everyone else, but let's be honest; I was nowhere near like everyone else. A lot of people might try to argue with this, but it's the truth.

I can remember Mom and I talking on the phone one afternoon when I got off work. This was a while after my transplant, probably close to *three years* after. I had just gotten an internship at Koch Industries, but was still struggling to stay healthy. I was also in grad school and in my last semester of college golf.

"Mom, what's wrong?" I said.

"Nothing...It's just this is nothing like I expected. This isn't normal. They keep saying that you're doing great, but it seems like you've been sick every two weeks. You have school and golf and work. How are you supposed to do all of those things if you're sick all the time?"

Again, I am not criticizing St. Luke's or their staff. They did a fantastic job and I am thankful to be alive. But unless you experience a heart transplant firsthand, unless you truly live the experience, you do not know what it is like. Period.

My immune system would never be the same. It had to stay suppressed in order for my heart to beat. That leads to my always being more apt to get sick. And I did. Oh, did I get sick! Within three years of my transplant, I had undergone two more additional surgeries due to my health. I had sinus surgery because of reoccurring sinus infections. I had my tonsils removed because I kept getting tonsillitis. It is very hard to hold a job, finish grad school, and play college golf when you are sick every week. But it's a fight that I had to face. It's a fight that I continue to battle every day. And that's not all.

Going through all of this is bound to spark all kinds of unproductive thoughts. Why me? Why did they die but I get to live? Was the alternative better? Did science keep me alive and I am actually supposed to be dead? But wouldn't you know it; they make a pill for that. They make a depression pill to go with all the other pills. Some of you may be familiar with antidepressants and their effects on the human body. It isn't a pretty sight. But try topping that off with 20-some other pills. Then try to live a normal life. Granted, my dosage and number of pills had dropped after a year, but I was still on a significant amount.

This was totally *normal* I was told. I was encouraged to seek the advice of counselors and any other professional that could help. There was one problem with that though. I am extremely stubborn. In my mind, how could some shrink help me with a problem they have never been through? Why in the hell would I listen to them?

I can remember one weekend I came home to Chanute and had a very emotional conversation with my parents about this. We argued back and forth until finally I got fed up with it all and just took off running. I had no idea where I was going or how long I was going to run. I just wanted to get away from it all. So many things happened so fast in my life that I had decided I had finally had enough.

As college continued, I would take the occasional drink of alcohol even though I knew I was supposed to limit myself. One drink turned to two and two drinks turned to five. Some nights I would even drink by myself. I was extremely lonely and it felt like my life had been taken away from me. I knew I had to do something fast or this great gift I had been given would be taken away.

Despite all this, there was one thing that stuck with me. My faith in Jesus Christ. I knew that everything was happening for a reason. I knew that eventually my life would turn around.

On February 18th, 2012, my life did just that. I was invited to give a speech at the Wichita Heart Ball hosted by the American Heart Association. This is a huge fundraising event that raises a lot of money each year and helps save many lives. All of the doctors throughout Wichita and the surrounding areas would be there. In fact, I would be giving a speech in front of Dr. Lloyd, the doctor who found my initial heart problem.

I suddenly began to realize just how lucky I was. I was a survivor. I had won the fight. The Heart Ball would be a perfect chance to share my story and encourage others to win whatever fights they were facing in their lives.

As the night approached, I became more and more excited. Whenever I get a chance to touch people's lives, I become very emotional. For me, this is my high. I used to think it was winning golf tournaments or maybe acing a test. But as time goes on, I've found that there is no better feeling than touching someone's life and bringing them closer to Christ.

I was extremely nervous. There would be a lot of important people at this event. It was very formal and even had a red carpet as you walked in. As I started talking to people and introducing myself, I became more and more at ease. When it came time to give my speech, I was ready. I thanked everyone for coming and went on to tell my story. As I glanced into the crowd, I could see my parents and a few doctors who had helped me along the way. I don't think there was a dry eye in the crowd.

When I finished, I thanked everyone for coming and encouraged them to donate money toward the fight against heart disease. Most importantly, I encouraged everyone to donate life. When it was all said and done, they raised over $326,000 dollars. Despite all my recent hardships, this would prove to be a great step forward in my fight back to life.

As the months went on, I did everything I could to stay positive. I worked out when I could and played golf as often as possible. One weekend I came home and was talking to my Dad about everything that had happened in my life. We got on the subject of depression and then started talking about my meds.

"Jeremy, those depression pills aren't good for you. I think you need to get off of those. It'll be hard at first, but I know you can do it. I promise you, you'll feel a lot better," Dad said.

I figured I would give it a try. I mean, what could it hurt? I trusted my dad with all my heart, and my mom agreed as well. I took all of those nasty pills out of my container and began my recovery.

It was hard. I started having mood swings and even more suicidal thoughts. I can't even begin to put into words what went through my head. I almost knew that this was going to be the end. But just when I thought it was all over, a little voice popped into my head.

"Do not fear, I am with you always."

It's funny how God works. I've learned that He will always answer your prayers; it just may not be the answer you want. God took me all the way down to rock bottom in order to lead me to the truth. As the antidepressants got out of my system, I got better and better. I began to realize why I was put on this earth. I began to realize my purpose.

We all have a cross to carry in life. Some are heavier than others, but none will ever be as heavy as the cross Jesus carried for us. And that is what keeps me going.

Our lives may not have turned out as we wanted or planned. I wanted to be a professional golfer, but God had other plans. The more we fight His plan, the more we will struggle. But as soon as we accept His plan for us, our lives will turn around. We will have a much better appreciation for life. That's exactly what happened to me.

As I learned to accept my condition and trust that the Lord would take care of me, my life continued to get better. Sure, I still had struggles, but the more I trusted in the Lord, the easier my life became.

I continued to play college golf, but approached it with a different outlook. When I stepped up on the tee, it wasn't about winning. It was about having fun and enjoying my second chance at life. The more I embraced this, the better I played.

Pretty soon two years had passed and I was getting ready to graduate college. It was hard to believe the years had flown by this fast. It seemed like just yesterday I had received the news about needing a heart. Nevertheless, I was ready to begin a new chapter in my life.

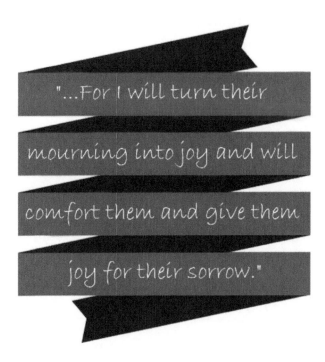

"...For I will turn their mourning into joy and will comfort them and give them joy for their sorrow."

Jeremiah 31:13

Chapter Ten

Bittersweet

---

few months before graduation, I got out of class and remembered that my Mom was supposed to send me a package in the mail. I had a little time before golf practice and figured I would go see if I had received anything. I opened the mailbox and I saw a few letters, but I didn't see a package anywhere. I was just about to throw the envelopes into my bag when one of them caught my eye.

When I saw what was on the envelope, I nearly lost it. I had waited so long for the moment I would receive a letter from my donor family. As I peeled back the seal, my hands began to shake. I opened the letter, took a deep breath, and began to read:

Dear Jeremy,

We received and read your letter some time ago, and want to send our apologies for taking such a long time to respond to it. As you can imagine, reading the letter was such a bitter-sweet thing to do, so many emotions as we read each line, knowing that while our son lost his life, you were able to be saved. We are so very glad to know that you are doing well, and able to live what we hope will be a very long and full life with much love and happiness.

Our Jeremy was such a sweet little boy, an ornery teenager, and grew up to be a very caring, loving young man and amazing father to his two children. Jeremy was an outdoor kind of guy, loved hunting, fishing, and taking his boat out whenever he could. He was a jokester and loved to laugh and have a good time, and could always make you smile on the worst of days. He was an awesome brother to his siblings, and actually seemed to enjoy being around them... for the most part :) If you needed help with anything, he was the first to offer a hand even for those tasks he KNEW he wasn't going to like.

He was a member of the Army National Guard and had been deployed right up until a week before his death. Upon returning home on emergency leave, he committed suicide due to PTSD. Getting the phone call saying that this had happened, and then seeing our child in a hospital bed and knowing he wasn't there anymore, was the hardest thing we will ever endure. While we knew donating his organs was the right thing to do and what he would have wanted, it was still a struggle. Ultimately we wanted something good to come from this tragedy...and knowing he was able to save lives does bring some comfort to our family.

I have been his 'bonus' mom for the past 20 years and there isn't one day that goes by that I don't think of him and wish he were here. My husband and I are raising his two children, and we will keep their daddy's memory alive to them through our pictures and stories of him... and tell them that he truly was a hero and saved lives including another young man who shares their daddy's name.

I wish you every happiness in the world, and hope you never feel any guilt because you are here living and breathing. This was God's plan for you so I believe you must truly be one special young man, and your parents are so very blessed to have you. I am sending you a big warm hug, from our family to you and asking that you cherish this life you have been given and never take anything for granted. Feel free to contact me again; I would love to hear how things are going, and that you are thriving in life...maybe eventually we can meet when we have moved through our grief a little more. Thank you for your letter; you will never know how much it means to all of us.

Sincerely,
Angie

There were a lot of times I doubted this was all a part of God's plan. There were a lot of times I doubted everything altogether. This letter though, this was something special. This letter confirmed that everything I had been through really was a part of something big.

Reading this letter was one of those experiences that words cannot describe. Knowing now that my new heart belonged to a soldier who shares my name is unreal. It hurts me to think about what he went through. It hurts me to think that he left this earth the way he did. But I know now that he is in a better place. I know that God needed a hero in heaven.

After reading the letter a few more times, I wiped away the tears and called my parents.

"Mom, Dad, I have something special to read to you guys. Are you busy?" I said.

"No, what is it?" Mom said.

"I got a letter back from my donor family," I said.

"Oh my gosh! Okay, let's hear it," Mom said.

I read the letter aloud to my parents. I could hear them beginning to break down. About halfway through, I began to cry and it took everything I had to finish the letter. I just couldn't get over the fact that my life had been saved by a soldier who shared my name. I also couldn't stop thinking about how hard it must have been for his family. What I went through was extremely difficult, but what his family went through is something I wouldn't wish on my worst enemy. Losing your son and then having to write a letter to the man who your son saved is a very extraordinary experience. I could only hope that one day I would get to show them that their Jeremy still lives on.

As the months passed, we exchanged letters a few more times and then began communicating by email. I would tell them what was going on in my life and they would share what was going on in theirs. Before long we had developed a close relationship and decided it was time to finally meet.

My girlfriend and I went on a Saturday morning. As each mile passed, I became more nervous. I was about to meet the family whose decision to donate Jeremy's organs three years ago saved my life. I was also about to meet the family who lost their soldier in such a tragic way three years ago. What would I say? How would it go?

We arrived around noon and stepped onto the front porch. We were greeted by the family with big hugs. We stepped inside and I immediately noticed pictures of Jeremy. I did everything I could to hold back the tears. It was a lot to take in at just 23 years-old, but I did my best.

As the afternoon progressed, we all began to get more comfortable with each other. We talked about a lot of things from memories of Jeremy to memories of my own. I did my best to tell them my story and they did their best to tell me his. They told me what a great kid he was and how he would never be forgotten. I told them how grateful I was and how thankful I was as well. Without them and their decision, I might not be here today.

Towards the end of our visit, we decided to take some pictures together. After that, I let them listen to my heart. Standing there as they listened was an experience I'll never forget. It wasn't just my heart. It was Jeremy's heart. A part of their Jeremy was still alive in me and that's what made it so special.

We said our goodbyes and promised each other that we would do it again real soon. I was a part of their family now and would do everything I could to bring as much joy to them as possible. We gave each other one last hug and cherished a day none of us will ever forget.

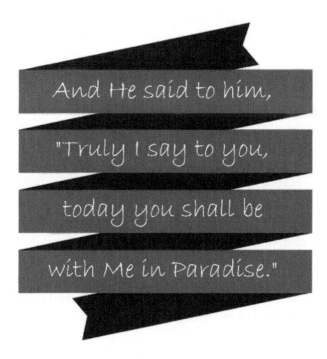

And He said to him,

"Truly I say to you,

today you shall be

with Me in Paradise."

Luke 23:43

Chapter Eleven

The Truth

Have you ever saved somebody's life? Have you ever prayed for somebody that was really sick or perhaps in their last few moments on earth? I can't say for sure whether I have saved anyone's life, but I do have one last story I would like to share with you.

I remember it plain as day. I was being wheeled to one of my tests and my wheelchair came to a sudden halt. Just as we were about to enter the elevator, people started yelling and told us to move back.

"Code blue! Code blue! Move!!" a doctor shouted.

"Clear!!" shouted another doctor as he zapped the flat-lined patient.

I had seen this on television before and I had even heard the code blue monitors going off in rooms beside me, but I had never encountered this firsthand. I felt so helpless. I wanted to help the guy desperately but what could I possibly do? It was at that moment my mind flashed back to an earlier childhood memory.

I was in the fourth grade and we were all lined up at the door waiting for the bell to ring. As my teacher opened the door, we heard the sound of an ambulance nearby.

"Class, let's bow our heads and say a Hail Mary for the soul on board that ambulance as well as their loved ones," my teacher said.

We were just young kids eager to get to recess. I doubt any of us knew what was going on. But why did that memory stick in my head ever since that day?

As the code blue patient entered the elevator, they zapped him once more and continued to give him oxygen. Just before the elevator doors closed, I began to recite the Hail Mary. As I prayed each word, I began to focus on the meaning and hoped that our Mother Mary would grant this man another chance. I prayed that if he didn't have Christ in his life, that maybe God would give him one more chance to come back to Him. I recited the Hail Mary a few more times and when the man finally disappeared from sight, I left the rest up to God.

A few days later as I was lying in bed, I noticed a man being wheeled past my room.

"Who is that?" I asked.

The nurse replied, "Do you remember that man we saw by the elevators that was in code blue? That is him. He is doing great!"

I had no idea the direction my life was going to take. I was a young college kid with big dreams and a great belief in the power of God. There were times when I questioned my second chance at life. There were times when I thought the alternative might have been better. Was I supposed to be dead and science saved me? Or was this really a part of God's plan?

These are all thoughts that went through my mind – they still do on occasion. It took me a long time to realize why this happened to me. It took me a long time to realize that this was God's plan for me.

No one said life was going to be easy or fun. At times it can be anything but that. I think back to the nights when I struggled the most. The nights when I felt like giving up for good. But every time that happened, I was reminded of all the struggles our Lord went through for us. Sending down your only son to die for our sins is the greatest sacrifice one could ever give. It was at those moments I knew I had to fight. It is at those moments we must continually pray for God's will and put all our trust in Him.

We are not put on this earth for happiness. This is not our paradise. I am telling you now, there is a much greater paradise awaiting us. We must simply open our eyes. Until we learn that our dreams mean nothing and that God means everything, we will never live a truly fulfilling life.

Some of you reading this may not believe in God. Or maybe you do, but it's been a while since you've been to church. Regardless, the thing that hurts me the most is seeing people who don't truly have God in their life. After seeing the impact He has had on my life and those around me, I don't want to see others die without Him in their lives. That is why I wrote this book. To share my story with others in hopes of bringing them closer to God.

I firmly believe that I was given a second chance to change people's lives through my story. I used to think I was supposed to be a professional golfer or maybe Mr. Universe, but I was given a much greater opportunity. God was shutting down my dreams not to discourage me, but to help me achieve and realize the ultimate dream of salvation in heaven. He was opening my eyes to something much greater than this life on earth.

I hope you have seen the impact God has had on my life and I hope you will begin to let Him into yours. One day we will all stand before God and He will look back on our lives. He will look at all the good things we have done and He will also look at all the times we turned our back to Him. He understands that we are sinners and will have mercy on us, but in the end I believe He will ask us one question. Did you try? – Win The Fight

"...to open their eyes so that they may turn from darkness to light and from the dominion of Satan to God,"

Acts 26:18

Appendix One

How My Experience Changed Others

Six months after my transplant, I decided to ask people who knew my story and followed me on Facebook a simple question. How has my experience changed/impacted your life? Immediately, story after story kept coming in. As I read them, tears came to my eyes. I had no idea how many lives I had changed. It was at that moment I decided to write this book in hopes of changing even more lives. The following are some of those stories:

Cassie Cleaver

> *From the moment that people in this community found out that you had been taken to Wichita, people instantly came together. The differences that were seen only the previous day seemed to have gone and everyone had a common goal and love. I saw each day how people would write wonderful scriptures and words to you on this page, some I had no idea about their faith,*

and they put it out there for everyone to see, something that maybe they hadn't done before or that was hard for them. I saw children color and draw hearts, wear bracelets and learn about what it is like to give of yourself for the betterment of someone else that you may not even know. So many people pulled strings and did so many things because they were inspired by you, your story and your faith. I personally have a kind of patience with my children and others that I didn't always have before. I was so closely reminded about how short life is and how things happen so randomly. I don't dwell on the small things anymore near as much. Thank you for reminding everyone about the true love that God has for each of us and how to be a great example of living your life through Him.

Robin Barker-Olberding

This year I had to renew my DL, for the first time, I'm an organ donor. You're the reason I chose to become an organ donor!

Teresa Hall

Jeremy, you have proven to me and so many others that with faith, love and support of friends and family you can move mountains. Also no matter how bad things are, to never give up. Your strength and faith have been truly amazing!!!!! I'm so proud and grateful you're my nephew, and thank God every day for blessing us with you.

Alicia Anderson

> *You strengthened my faith in God and in all the people. You are the spirit of life in my eyes. I hope that nothing ever changes in your life to make you bitter and say why me?*

Jodi Lucke

> *You, and your family, displayed such courage and faith at a time when life was out of control and your destiny uncertain. You also reminded all of us to live every day, because we never know what tomorrow will bring. You have shown us having it all isn't in what you "have", but knowing what you have is all you need.*

Karen Graham

> *Jeremy, you have impacted my life by showing me the power of faith–faith in family, faith in God and faith in community. Your family drew on its strength to get through your diagnosis and transplant and continues to be strong in your journey. Your faith in God never wavered. You believed he had a purpose for you and I believe it too. You were meant to touch lives and you have and continue to do so. You brought an entire community together. You have changed many lives and you have only just begun. Thank you for who you are!*

Dawn Greenwood Allen

> *I donated my blood for the first time....now I've done it twice! I have been an organ donor for*

*a few years and John and I argued about it.
Now, because of what you have been through,
he says he understands why I am!*

Amy Kneeland Madison

*I think it is awesome that I know someone
that was personally picked by God to spread
the message about donating organs. I thought
having it labeled on your driver's license was
enough, so glad to know better now. May
you continue your journey with more great
check-ups and many blessings to you and your
wonderful family!*

Shanna Guiot

*Renewed awe and respect for your whole
family, but most importantly I found myself
talking about organ donation to many, many
people. I have always been a donor (on my DL)
and have always encouraged everyone I know
to do the same ... but now it has impacted our
whole community and I have a real story to tell
about a great guy whose life was saved. Thanks
to God for giving the doctors and scientists the
knowledge to do such AMAZING things!!!*

Lisa Gant

*Jeremy, I first just want to say that you are an
amazing son! I could not have been blessed
with a better son. You have taught me so much
through everything we have been through. Your
faith is just amazing, you are such a fighter*

and I am confident that is why God chose you! He has great plans for you, I just know it. You have pulled this community together and you have taught so many of us to never take life for granted as we know not what awaits us. You have so many people that look up to you and respect you. You have truly been an inspiration to many. My wish for you is a long, happy and healthy life as there is no one who deserves it more. I also just want you to know that your dad and I thank God everyday for our second chance with our son! We Love You with all our hearts Jeremy, Love Mom and Dad.

Debbie S-Claing

I'm so glad you are doing well and back to doing things you never thought possible.. able to BREATH again and walk to the bathroom without being exhausted..:) My husband had a Heart Transplant on Oct. 21, 2009 and it has changed ...our life for the better.. NO REJECTIONS to this day.. It's so inspiring to read success stories of others.. Congratulations Sweetheart.. Hope you have MANY MANY YEARS of health and happiness.

Shelly Kingery

What an amazing young man you are, I have known for many years you were going to be an awesome young man.... but I didn't know how truly awesome you were led to be. Your strength, dedication, integrity, and overall the way you choose to live your life is what has changed my life the most. As you know, I have 4 sons and for them to call you a role model is a blessing for me. Who you are and what you have endured has changed my family's life forever. I know at times you wish to forget all you have been faced with; however I want you to know God has given you a special gift–the gift to be a role model for our young. Thank you for who you are, but a special thank you for being a positive role model for our children.

Herman-Elaine Colvin

I believe your trial has been evidence of the power of prayer to multitudes. It was amazing to watch the mushroom effect of supporters on your Facebook as we all rallied together to support you in prayer and to know that God offered us an opportunity to see His grace at work not only in our church, but in our entire community.

Linda Wolken

I've learn that the power of prayer can make a miracle happen. To see you and your Mom & Dad in church smiling again is enough to make me feel so good, that they will be able to see you go on with your future and love you the way that parents should love their children. Good luck Jeremy with going back with your golfing, you make everyone so proud that you are still here with us...Sending our love to you and your Parents...God Bless You!

Julie White Stewart

*Jeremy- You gave me hope for your genera-
tion. When you asked us not to pray for a heart
but to pray for God's will for you, I was like,
WOW! He's a young kid and he gets it! To see
the younger generation stand for what they
believe in and allow us to see their faith gives
us all inspiration! I am just in awe of how well
you are doing and so thankful! May God bless
you and give you guidance all of your days! :-)*

"Do not withhold good from those who deserve it, when it is in your power to act."

Proverbs 3:27

Appendix Two

The Importance of Donating Life

A lot of people don't know the true importance of donating life. I was an organ donor before, but I would never know just how important it was until a donor saved my life. Let me tell you a story of something that happened not too long ago. It had been more than a year since my transplant and I had just turned 21. My license expired so I had to go to the DMV and get a new one. I was pretty pumped because in Kansas you get a horizontal license on your 21st birthday instead of the vertical one you get as a teenager. I usually go to the DMV in Chanute, but it just so happened I was in Wichita at college and had to get it there. When I arrived, I noted that the building was four times the size of the one in Chanute. Even worse, there had to be close to a hundred people standing around. "Grab a number and stand in line!" the lady behind the desk shouted. "Hmm..." I thought, "this is different."

When my number was finally called, I walked up to the long counter and gave them my old license and card I had gotten in the mail. As I answered all the questions, she asked me if I would like to remain an organ donor. I smiled and gave an immediate yes. About that time, I happened to hear the gentleman beside me get asked the same question.

"Sir, would you like to be an organ donor?" the lady asked him.

"No, that's okay," he replied.

If I had heard that before, I probably wouldn't have thought anything of it. This time, I was devastated. I wanted to go up to the guy and yell, "What the hell are you doing?!" Some of you reading this may still be wondering what the big deal is, so I want you to read these facts I've listed below. This should give you a pretty good idea as to why I was so let down.

- ♥ One organ donor can save up to eight lives. The same donor can also save or improve the lives of up to 50 people by donating tissues and eyes.
- ♥ Approximately 18 people die each day awaiting a life-saving organ transplant.
- ♥ A new name is added to the national waiting list every ten minutes.
- ♥ Only slightly more than 50 percent of people on the waiting list will receive an organ within five years.
- ♥ In 2010, there were over two million deaths in the U.S. Imagine if all of them had been organ donors.
- ♥ Most major religions in the U.S. support organ donation.
- ♥ There is no cost to donors or their families for organ or tissue donation.

I hope you see now why donating life is so important. Each number you just read represents a life, whether it is a mom, a dad, a brother, a sister or even a child. Imagine if my donor hadn't chosen to donate his organs. I may not have lived to write this book. I can only hope that the guy standing beside me at the DMV will read this book and have a change of heart. I encourage all of you to go online or to your local DMV and register to become an organ donor. I guarantee you will feel better about yourself knowing that when you die, your organs might save lives like mine.

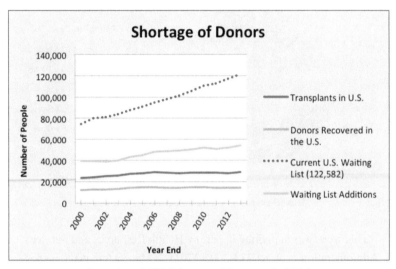

Based on OPTN data as of January 3, 2014

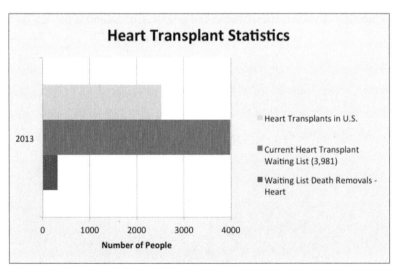

Based on OPTN data as of May 16, 2014

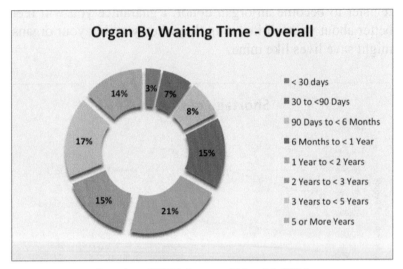

Based on OPTN data as of May 16, 2014

"This work was supported in part by Health Resources and Services Administration contract 234-2005-37011C. The content is the responsibility of the authors alone and does not necessarily reflect the views or policies of the Department of Health and Human Services, nor does mention of trade names, commercial products, or organizations imply endorsement by the U.S. Government."

Photos

Before The Transplant

*Celebrating after winning
the Kansas Junior Amateur*

*Hitting a shot in a tournament one
year before the transplant*

Senior picture with all of my trophies

Posing a few months before the transplant

Tom Watson & me in the hospital

After The Transplant

Jeremy Gant
#474
10-11-10

*My picture on the wall at St Luke's
after transplant*

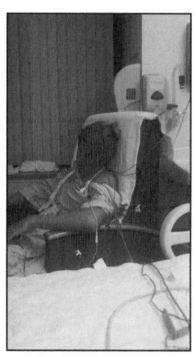

*Sitting up right after the
transplant*

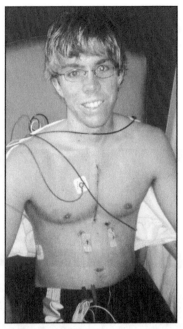

Smiling a few days after the transplant

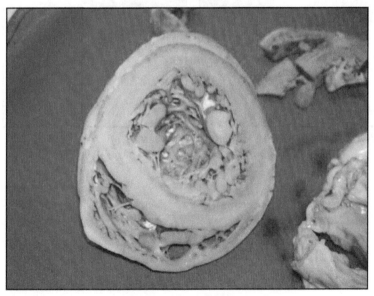

Picture of my old heart

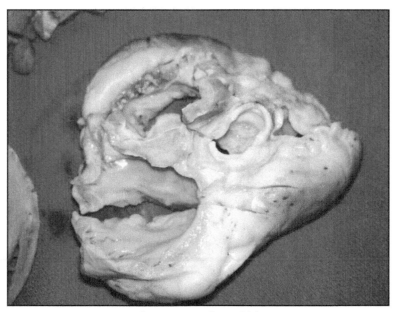

Another picture of my old heart

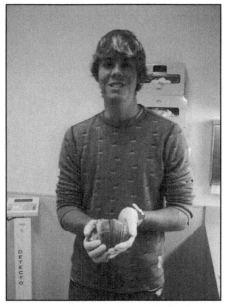

Holding my old heart

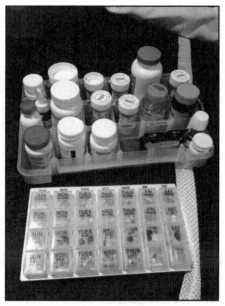

*The medicine I now have to take
every day*

Rickie Fowler & me at Karsten Creek

Holding a catfish

Lifting weights at home

The Newman University golf team at the Jeremy Gant Heart Classic

Local supporters wearing "Heart Fore Jeremy" shirts

Local restaurant celebrating the news of my new heart

Grandma & Grandpa at Jeremy Gant Heart Classic

Newspaper article featuring
Coach McGraw & myself

My hero, Jeremy

Notes

"Statistics," Donate Life, accessed May 8, 2014, http://donatelife.net/statistics/

"Facts about Organ Donation," New York Organ Donor Network, accessed May 8, 2014, http://www.donatelifeny.org/about-donation/quick-facts-about-donation/

"The Need Is Real: Data," U.S. Department of Health & Human Services, accessed May 8, 2014, http://www.organdonor.gov/about/data.html

"Waiting For Your Transplant," Transplant Living, accessed May 8, 2014, http://www.transplantliving.org/before-the-transplant/waiting-for-your-transplant/

"Learn The Facts," U.S. Department of Health & Human Services, accessed May 8, 2014, http://organdonor.gov/whydonate/facts.html

CPSIA information can be obtained at www.ICGtesting.com
Printed in the USA
LVOW01s1253300614

392323LV00001B/1/P